Speech Acts in Blake's *Milton*

Using a framework based on J. L. Austin's understanding of performative speech and Angela Esterhammer's work on how things are done with words in Milton's and Blake's poetry, this book provides an extended close reading of the speech acts of characters in Blake's epic poem *Milton*. With the exception of what we learn about in the part of the poem known as the Bard's Song, Blake's *Milton* is dedicated to providing an incredibly detailed account of the numerous facets of the instant of time immediately prior to apocalypse, an instant in which Milton is the protagonist, and Blake himself a participant. This study explores how in the poem sacred history proceeds towards and through the instant by means of the speech act. This extended commentary is intended for not just Blake scholars but also the common reader who wishes to approach Blake's brief epic for the first time. For scholars, this monograph offers a full account of a crucial but previously unexplored theme in the scholarship about *Milton*. For the common reader, it offers a comprehensive introduction to what Northrop Frye called 'one of the most gigantic imaginative achievements in English poetry'.

Brian Russell Graham is a two-time graduate of the University of Glasgow, where he completed an M.A. (Hons.) and PhD in English Literature. He is currently a lecturer at the University of Copenhagen and Copenhagen Business School. His first monograph, *The Necessary Unity of Opposites*, published in 2011, is a study of Northrop Frye, particularly Frye's dialectical thinking. His second monograph, *On a Common Culture*, was published in 2022.

Routledge Focus on Literature

Female Physicians in American Literature
Abortion in 19th-Century Literature and Culture
Margaret Jay Jessee

Masculinities in Post-Millennial Popular Romance
Eirini Arvanitaki

A Glimpse at the Travelogues of Baghdad
Iman Al-Attar

Shakespeare in the Present
Political Lessons under Biden
Philip Goldfarb Styrt

Speech Acts in Blake's *Milton*
Brian Russell Graham

Literature, Education, and Society
Bridging the Gap
Charles F. Altieri

Shakespeare and the Theater of Pity
Shawn Smith

Trauma, Memory and Silence of the Irish Woman in Contemporary Literature
Wounds of the Body and the Soul
Edited by Madalina Armie and Verónica Membrive

For more information about this series, please visit: www.routledge.com/Routledge-Focus-on-Literature/book-series/RFLT

Speech Acts in Blake's *Milton*

Brian Russell Graham

NEW YORK AND LONDON

First published 2023
by Routledge
605 Third Avenue, New York, NY 10158

and by Routledge
4 Park Square, Milton Park, Abingdon, Oxon, OX14 4RN

Routledge is an imprint of the Taylor & Francis Group, an informa business

© 2023 Brian Russell Graham

The right of Brian Russell Graham to be identified as author of this work has been asserted in accordance with sections 77 and 78 of the Copyright, Designs and Patents Act 1988.

All rights reserved. No part of this book may be reprinted or reproduced or utilised in any form or by any electronic, mechanical, or other means, now known or hereafter invented, including photocopying and recording, or in any information storage or retrieval system, without permission in writing from the publishers.

Trademark notice: Product or corporate names may be trademarks or registered trademarks, and are used only for identification and explanation without intent to infringe.

Library of Congress Cataloging-in-Publication Data
Names: Graham, Brian Russell, author.
Title: Speech acts in Blake's Milton / Brian Russell Graham.
Description: New York, NY : Routledge, 2023. |
Series: Routledge focus on literature | Includes bibliographical references and index.
Identifiers: LCCN 2022032741 (print) | LCCN 2022032742 (ebook) | ISBN 9781032379180 (hardback) | ISBN 9781032379197 (paperback) | ISBN 9781003342571 (ebook)
Subjects: LCSH: Blake, William, 1757-1827. Milton. | Speech acts (Linguistics) in literature. | LCGFT: Literary criticism.
Classification: LCC PR4144.M63 G73 2023 (print) | LCC PR4144.M63 (ebook) | DDC 821/.7--dc23/eng/20220831
LC record available at https://lccn.loc.gov/2022032741
LC ebook record available at https://lccn.loc.gov/2022032742

ISBN: 978-1-032-37918-0 (hbk)
ISBN: 978-1-032-37919-7 (pbk)
ISBN: 978-1-003-34257-1 (ebk)

DOI: 10.4324/9781003342571

Typeset in Times New Roman
by MPS Limited, Dehradun

To the Association of Literary Scholars, Critics and Writers

Contents

Introduction   1

1 The Bard's Song I: From the Beginning Until the
   Creation of Fallen Space   18

2 The Bard's Song II: The Creation of Fallen Time
   and Death, and Milton's Response to the Song   34

3 'the forward path/Of Milton's journey' and the
   Opponents of His Progress   52

4 Opposition to Milton in Golgonooza and Los's
   Defence of the 'Shadow Terrible'   65

5 The Descent of Ololon   91

6 The Redemption of the Contraries   103

7 Coda: *Milton* as Speech Act   119

   Bibliography   124
   Index   126

Introduction

Although there are exceptions to the rule, as we shall see, everything that happens in Blake's Prophetic Books either results in progress towards apocalypse or serves to frustrate that process, whether by deepening the Fall or bolstering the (fallen) *status quo*. This is as true of *Milton* as it is of Blake's other prophecies, but *Milton* is different from what Blake wrote earlier in his career, with the possible exception of *Europe*. As numerous Blake scholars have pointed out, the events of the poem, with the exception of what we learn about in the *analepsis* represented by the Bard's Song, are the contents of a single instant. So, what gets related by the poem is a historical sequence followed by an incredibly detailed account of the numerous facets of an instant of time. From one perspective, the chronology no longer applies and the events of the Bard's Song and the developments of the instant all belong to the same 'structure' – a point I shall return to in the very last section of this study – but for the best part I will discuss the poem as a history, specifically a sacred history, which concludes with the instant, immediately prior to apocalypse, which most of the poem is dedicated to providing an account of.

The poem is partly about the visions of Blake the character in the poem (the intradiegetic Blake). Those visions are *parts of* the instant. That visionary experience is clearly twofold. It comprises what Blake witnesses in Felpham, when, after Ololon's descent, Milton descends, defeats Satan and unites with Ololon. But it also comprises Blake's vision of Golgonooza, which he experiences when he arrives there as part of a character complex also comprising Los and Milton. Of interest to us, especially towards the end of this commentary, is the relationship between Blake's visionary experience and, first, the rest of the instant, and, second, the events of the Bard's Song.

DOI: 10.4324/9781003342571-1

2 *Introduction*

Fox is the commentator who speaks most persuasively of the 'instant'. She argues that everything that happens in the poem (if we exclude the Bard's Song) happens at exactly the same 'instant':

> I have chosen the word "instant" as the time reference of the actions of the poem in order to distinguish that reference from Blake's broader, more inclusive conception, "moment". The events of *Milton*, I must emphasize, are not simultaneous because they all occur within that paradoxical moment which is at once seven thousand years long and as brief as a poet's sudden inspiration. They are not, that is, simultaneous because time is irrelevant to them, because they occur beyond or within the calibrations of time. They are simultaneous because each occurs at the same precise "instant" of that moment, the same minute, calibrated segment of that seven-thousand-year period that comprises fallen history. All the actions of the poem occur in the last measurable segment of the moment, the last fragment of time itself, the instant before apocalypse puts an end to time. (1976: 18)

She argues that even if it appears as though a sequence emerges in the poem, the action is free of any genuine sequences. Blake's task is to '[describe] each individual facet of the event, establishing the congruency of each new facet with the previous ones by demonstrating, usually through repetition of key images, that they have the same history and the same effect' (1976: 98) or in each case to analyze the 'different aspects of that timeless event' (1976: 89). Fox does concede that, in Book II, a sequence emerges. She views this sequence as paradox, however, because the effect of a sequence is only generated by the shifting perspective of the poem:

> we see Ololon pass through the polypus into Blake's garden seeking Milton, whereupon he appears; then we see Milton's resistance of the satanic lure, and Ololon's symbolic division from Rahab; then Milton's redefinition of that resistance in terms of fallen reality, and Ololon's literalization of her division; finally the consummation implied in each of these dramatic scenes is realized in the conversion of the Starry Eight to Jesus. There is clearly a sequence here, but it is a paradoxical sequence in which any individual stage of it contains it all: Ololon's descent into the polypus is her union with Milton, for it makes them coextensive; their resistance of their satanic portions is their union, because those annihilable states were all that prevented that union; the literalization of the resistance only clarifies it as it

relates to life on this earth of vegetation; the consummation in the figures of angels and Jesus has been implicit all along, for the angels have been with Milton since he descended, and Jesus has been with Ololon since she descended. (1976: 184)

In what follows, the focus is on the instances of agency characterizing the action of the poem, whether it is actions related in the Bard's Song or in the remainder of the poem and therefore the 'instant', and whether the instance of agency results in progress towards apocalypse or frustrates that process. Of great significance is the fact that the instances of agency in the poem involve no use of physical force; they feature no epic-type conflict or violence, or even much physical action. In the Bard's Song, which is where the action starts, tempers certainly flare, but there is no violence. Indeed, a court or assembly is brought down to adjudicate in the conflict between Palamabron and Satan. There is a reaction from Satan when the verdict goes against him, but no physical conflict. There is nothing physically threatening about either Los's sons or the sons of Luvah when they encounter the Los-Milton-Blake complex, and Los, for his part, relies on the power of speech: the sons want to throw Milton into the Fires, but Los rules it out. His speech is about the importance of *waiting* 'till the Judgement is past' (25.59, E122).[1]

One episode, it is true, involves physical combat. 'Milton', explains Damon, 'had placed Reason as the chief of man's faculties (*PL* v-102); therefore in Blake's *Milton*, Urizen is the basis of Milton's philosophy and his outstanding difficulty' (1988: 423). Unlike the other characters who oppose Milton in Book I, Urizen's resistance is non-verbal and physical. Urizen encounters Milton in two different settings, and clay is important in both settings. In the first, Urizen seems to overpower Milton: clay is turned into marble, and Milton is pictured first with his feet trapped in marble, and then walking on the marble, his feet bleeding (19.3–4, E112). But in the second setting, which is perhaps visualized in the design of plate 15, Milton is a match for Urizen[2]. The setting is primarily the river Arnon, but the location is a composite place: the Arnon is combined with a number of Biblical locations, each of which is relevant because of its scriptural connotations. (Mahanaim, for example, is where Jacob wrestles with God.) Urizen pours the icy fluid of the river Jordan onto Milton's brain, trying to assimilate Milton to his decadent Urizenic worldview. But in this setting Milton can use the 'red clay of Succoth'. As Frye points out, Genesis includes an account of creation in which Adam is made from the earth or clay (the *adamah*) (2006: 127). In an action which reminds us of this creation myth, Milton uses clay to create for Urizen a 'human form':

> Urizen emerged from his Rocky Form & from his Snows,
> And he also darkend his brows: freezing dark rocks between
> The footsteps. and infixing deep the feet in marble beds:
> That Milton labourd with his journey, & his feet bled sore
> Upon the clay now chang'd to marble; also Urizen rose,
> And met him on the shores of Arnon; & by the streams of the brooks
>
> Silent they met, and silent strove among the streams, of Arnon
> Even to Mahanaim, when with cold hand Urizen stoop'd down
> And took up water from the river Jordan: pouring on
> To Miltons brain the icy fluid from his broad cold palm.
> But Milton took of the red clay of Succoth, moulding it with care
> Between his palms: and filling up the furrows of many years
> Beginning at the feet of Urizen, and on the bones
> Creating new flesh on the Demon cold, and building him,
> As with new clay a Human form in the Valley of Beth Peor.
> (18.51–19.14, E112)

On this level Milton will be unable to proceed. The two struggle with one another throughout, though towards the end of the poem, when Milton is confronting Satan (the fallen Urizen), we learn that, on the other plane, Milton is victorious over Urizen (39.53–54, E141).

Whether the instance of agency results in progress towards apocalypse or frustrates that process, in *Milton*, things are done with words.[3] As James observes,

> Though like most epics *Milton* does contain battles and journeys, both of these, like other crucial events in the poem, take place and are resolved in a mode that is primarily verbal. ... Each crisis point is typically marked, not by trial of strength, but by "debate" in which characters pit against each other dramatizations of self and the world-views with which they identify. (1976: 90)

In Book I, our interest is partly on Los's speeches to his own sons and, subsequently, the sons of Luvah. In Book II, our focus is partly Milton's successfully defeating Satan and enlightening Ololon through the power of speech. But it is not only Los and Milton who do things with words in the poem. Opponents of the allies of mankind rely on the power of words, too. In the Bard's Song, Satan deceives Los through verbal manipulation, for example. Equally importantly, at times what is crucial to the action is that a performative speech act proves *ineffective*. In some cases, the focus is on a failed speech act on the part of an opponent figure: think of Rahab and

Tirzah's unsuccessful use of words to tempt Milton's redeemed self or Satan's ineffective final speech to Milton towards the end of the poem. At other times, the focus is on the failure of the speech act of a character allied to mankind: Los's failed attempt to rule out Satan's driving the Harrow is an example.

The division in the nature of the speech suggests all speech in the poem is characterized by a moral antithesis, and up to a point it is. That said, the nature of a particular speech act is really identified by what Austin calls the perlocutionary effect, and when we judge the impact of a speech act in relation to the perlocutionary effect, we often move beyond the scope of the *intention* of the speech act. Milton's response to the Bard's Song – his response is one of several perlocutionary effects – has little to do with the intention of the Song.

Additionally, in a small number of instances a speech act is dual in nature: it simultaneously deepens the Fall, but also creates the conditions for the ultimate restoration. We'll turn to this factor in Chapter 2 when considering how the Eternals react to the Satan's perfidy.

Subcategories of Speech Act in *Milton*

Three subcategories of speech act are discernible in the poem. To a significant extent, the interest turns on characters' *agonistic* verbal exchanges in Blake's *Milton*. The Bard's Song is full of verbal conflict. Next, the zoas verbally resist Milton when he descends. Then, in the course of the journey to Golgonooza undertaken by Los-Blake-Milton, Los's sons wage a war of words on Los-Blake-Milton, which Los responds to in combative speeches. Subsequently, they encounter the sons of Luvah, and agonistic speeches are exchanged once more. At the end of the poem, Milton and Satan agonistically address each other, Milton defeating Satan through combative speech.

Blake has in mind a battle of ideas, on the one hand, and actual war, on the other; the two are utterly distinct, and he is entirely in favour of the former and entirely against the latter. The former is more akin to what in the poem is cast as the 'Wars of Man ... in Great Eternity' (34.50, E134). Actual war is of course associated with our world; intellectual warfare is an activity of Eden, Blake's heaven or apocalyptic world, and it is associated with the 'Divine Family'. This opposition crops up in *Jerusalem* as well as *Milton*. In *Jerusalem* the Divine Family states that

> Our wars are wars of life, & wounds of love,
> With intellectual spears, & long winged arrows of thought:
> Mutual in one anothers love and wrath all renewing
> We live as One Man (34.14–17, E180)

In *Milton*, Ololon contrasts Ulro with Eden, when the former world heaves into view. She is struck by the stark contrast between how things are in eternity and how they are in Ulro. The 'Wars of Man' appear in a parodic form in Ulro, which means that they are connected to death. In Eternity, War and Hunting are intellectual and creative endeavours; in Ulro the two activities which go by those names are parodies of eternal activities. (We shall return to Ololon's thoughts in Chapter 5.)

Blake's emphasis on verbal agonism is also tied in with a literary form. Traditional epics promote war, as Blake argues in 'On Homers Poetry': 'The Classics, it is the Classics! & not Goths nor Monks, that Desolate Europe with Wars' (E270). Blake's epic will be Hebraic rather than Hellenic, even if the great epics were Hellenic. Blakean epic emphasizes victory, like the classics, but it stresses non-violence and speech. In 'On Virgil', Blake insists that the Bible and by extension 'the Hebraic' are free of the idealization of war:

> Sacred Truth has pronounced that Greece & Rome as Babylon & Egypt: so far from being parents of Arts & Sciences as they pretend: were destroyers of all Art. Homer Virgil & Ovid confirm this opinion & make us reverence The Word of God, the only light of antiquity that remains unperverted by War (E270)

That Blake's epic rejects violence and throws the emphasis onto speech also marks it out as Biblical in this specific sense.[4]

But it would be wrong to start out with the impression that *all* important speech in the poem is agonistic. A great deal of speech is non-combative. Mental revolution can also be precipitated by speech which is simply enlightening. We have the Seven Angels' enlightening Milton, and Milton's enlightening Ololon. Luetha's long speech in the Bard's Song also falls into this category. She does not engage in conflict with the Assembly; rather, she informs them and pleads with them.

Additionally, soliloquies, where there is no addressee at all, play a significant role in Blake's epic. Strikingly, a number of soliloquies possess performative power, and speeches of that kind, quite surprisingly, also play a part in the progress towards apocalypse. The speeches in question will be discussed in detail, but they include, Milton's soliloquy when he decides to descend, Los's self-identifying soliloquy when he has joined with Blake and Milton, and Ololon's soliloquies over the course of her descent.

Critical Background

The conception of the speech act is the organizing idea of what follows. On one level, a theory can be applied to any literary text. It has been said that when working with speech act theory, two kinds of speech acts are germane, and that while a focus on one kind of speech act directs our attention to lyrical poetry, another kind of focus draws our attention to novels and plays. Thus, speech act theory can be applied to virtually all kinds of literature. But the present study is not animated by an *a priori* interest in speech act theory and therefore an insistence on using the theory at every opportunity. Speech act theory is especially appropriate for Blake's *Milton*. Blake's epic involves no siege of Troy, no militarism in heaven; everything is achieved through speech.

Nor would it be true to say that in what follows a single school of criticism has been adopted at the expense of other approaches. This study draws on the heritage of Blake scholarship. What Frye says about the steady progress of criticism, on the one hand, and deconstruction, on the other, sums up the situation admirably:

> Every teacher of the humanities employed by a university is expected to be a "productive scholar", and in the present state of criticism not everyone can be that. It follows that there have to be critical methods developed, including my own in its narrower aspect, which enable scholars to produce what are primarily academic exercises, not really increasing the understanding of literature as a whole but demonstrating a certain competence in the subject. There remains however a genuinely "productive" group, who, though operating in a variety of "schools", seem to me to have, for all their surface disagreements, an underlying consensus of attitude, out of which a progress toward some unified comprehension of the subject could emerge, and lead to a construction far more significant than any deconstruction of it could possibly be. (1990: xviii)

What is striking about the practice stemming from such first principles is not that it undervalues more recent scholarship: no such built-in prejudice can be fairly accorded to it. Rather, it is that the practice in question is more thorough in its search through the critical legacy for work that endures. As such, it is certainly an approach which takes a low view of what C.S. Lewis calls 'chronological snobbery' – an *a priori* preference for the most recent. In what follows, the reader will quickly realize that my engagement with earlier decades of scholarship about Blake is substantial.[5] Today, it is perhaps still uncontroversial to make substantial use of Frye's *magnum opus*; across the decades, most commentators have felt that there is much to be learned from Frye's first book. In a 2012 publication, Morris Eaves, casting his mind back to the 2007 Blake conference held in York, observes that a significant number of attendees 'identified Northrop Frye's *Fearful Symmetry* as the primary and positive twentieth-century landmark' (2012: 225).[6] And that constituency remains sizable today. That I hold in high regard works of Blake scholarship from the 1970s may be more surprising, but it shouldn't be. Three of the four monographs about Blake's *Milton* – my own volume is only the fifth monograph about the poem – were written in the seventies, and they are fine works of literary criticism, Fox's especially. (Wittreich's *Angel of Apocalypse*, his monograph about Blake's view of Milton, also dates from that decade). The *scale* of these works, combined with their quality, should mean they can be used substantively and profitably in any given critical work about Blake's *Milton*.

This study works with a range of commentaries about Blake, but one category *is* of prime importance. Works focused on Blake and language represent a special group of secondary works. Works focused on Blake and *other* concerns are of great relevance to what follows and they are used throughout, but, unlike works focused on language, these studies impact a study about Blake and language like cross-currents.

A small number of sources in the former category represent the key sources in what follows in that they impact directly on the main argument of this commentary. James's simple observation about how speeches represent the main action of the poem make him an essential source. The works of two other Blake scholars – Susan Fox and Angela Esterhammer – also provide key structuring ideas for what follows, and we should proceed by discussing their contributions.

Angela Esterhammer

Over the past few decades, a number of commentators have drawn attention to the *performative* nature of Blake's poetry, whether it's the poems themselves or how Blake's characters use language. Linguists such as Taylor and Middleton were amongst the first to begin the process of teasing out the performative nature of Blake's poetic idiom, and the performative nature of Blake's language is a theme in Essick's *William Blake and the Language of Adam*. The most significant achievement in this area of Blake scholarship is Angela Esterhammer's *Creating States: Studies in the Performative Language of John Milton and William Blake*.

Introduction 9

In her study, Esterhammer distinguishes between two types of performative in Blake as well as Milton – the sociopolitical and the phenomenological:

> sociopolitical refers to an utterance which more or less explicitly derives performative force from the speaker's (and audience's) position within a societal institution (the church, the law, the class system), as well as a mode of interpretation which analyses performative utterances by appeal to historical, political, or institutional circumstances. But literary critics also use the term "performative" in a different sense, to refer to an author's ability to "create" reality through poetic or fictional utterance, independently of societal conventions but in accordance with literary conventions that ascribe creative (or visionary, or prophetic) authority to the speaking voice and elicit the reader's or hearer's assent. This type of utterance, and the corresponding interpretive approach, is here called the phenomenological performative, since its concern is the positing of phenomena whose existence is determined, not by historical reality, but by some other set of criteria. (1994: 12)

In connection with the latter, Esterhammer, making a significant contribution to speech act theory, suggests such speech is characterized by a kind of performativity akin to that of the divine word:

> the recurrent paradigm for the phenomenological performative, in speech-act theory and in visionary poetry, is divine creation by the word. If performative utterances in poetry do not create phenomena of the same order as does the divine word, they may nevertheless lay claim to a similar type of performativity: non-conventional, extra-societal, deriving from the will or intentionality of the speaker alone. (1994: 13)

Esterhammer doesn't allude to Frye in this context, but his distinction between works of literature which are plot-organized and works which are theme-organized is highly apposite. She acknowledges that it is conventional to connect the sociopolitical with fiction and the phenomenological with lyrical poetry: critics typically limit their interest in sociopolitical performatives to novels, where we are shown characters' social selves verbally interacting with one another according to pre-existing power relations, whereas the commentator interested in the phenomenological performative will turn to forms in which the poet creates his own world, Romantic poetry, for example, but also lyrical poetry more generally. But Esterhammer aims to move beyond the notion that the two different kinds of speech act are limited to corresponding kinds of literary texts. She is of the view that the same text can be discussed in terms of both types of performative. Indeed, her intention goes beyond that: ultimately, her aim is to suggest that we should think of these two kinds of speech act as features of the same speech act:

> my attempt in this book is to bring the two speech-act approaches together, not by eliding differences, but by demonstrating how the sociopolitical performative and the phenomenological performative interact in specific texts, with or without the author's awareness that this is happening. The two types of performatives may appear in confrontation with one another, the poet trying to oppose or resist the discourse of institutions with a speech act that derives authority from private visionary consciousness. They may also converge within the same utterance, since language, even when used with a conscious appeal to visionary tradition, is necessarily implicated in, perhaps limited by, contemporary social and political discourses. (1994: 25)

To turn to what all of this means for Blake scholarship, without discounting the relevance to Blake's poetry of the idea of the constative speech act, Esterhammer suggests we develop critical sensitivity to the two kinds of performative utterance in Blake's poetry. No doubt we should have a critical eye for phenomenological performatives in connection with the text as a speech act, and sociopolitical performatives in connection with speech acts in the text, but Esterhammer urges us to go beyond that level of awareness. We should aim to develop critical awareness of how these two performatives can be combined in the same utterance, she argues. It may well be that we will find that we need to keep these two kinds of performative apart when dealing with Blake's earlier poetry, but Esterhammer suggests that, while in Blake's earlier poetry the two kinds of performative are to a fair degree separate from one another, in both his shorter and longer prophecies the two are fully integrated:

> While *Songs of Innocence and of Experience* presents an idealized form of this distinction, even in these poems the "innocence" of individual expression is threatened by societal discourse, and in Blake's later poetry it becomes increasingly more difficult to draw a dividing line between the two kinds of performative language. (1995: 124)

Consequently, when working with Blake's Prophetic Books, *Milton* included, we should adopt a nuanced approach to performatives, considering not just the phenomenological performatives connected to the text itself and the sociopolitical performatives represented by speech in the text, but also the phenomenological dimension of sociopolitical speech, and vice versa.

Esterhammer is an essential source in what follows, but while I employ her important distinction between phenomenological and sociopolitical, this opposition is not the *organizing* opposition of my analysis. 'The Nature of my Work is Visionary or Imaginative', said Blake: 'it is an Endeavour to Restore what the Ancients call'd the Golden Age' (E555). In and of itself, Esterhammer's concept of the phenomenological performative carries no sense of whether the performative brings humanity closer to apocalypse or whether it frustrates that progress. When the judgement goes against him in the Bard's Song, Satan's performative speech alters reality; towards the end of the poem, Milton's speech to Satan, as well as his exchanges with Ololon, plays a key role in taking the world to the very edge of apocalypse. It should be incontestable that we need a vocabulary which *separates* such contrasting phenomenological performatives. Esterhammer's distinction, then, while it is useful, will be integrated into the framework for speech acts I elaborated earlier in this introduction.

Susan Fox

Esterhammer usefully observes that Austin's categories do not necessarily divide a single speech act into three separate acts; rather, they represent the 'three perspectives from which any utterance may be considered' (1995: 4). But we must go much further when dealing with speech acts in *Milton*: all the speech acts are aspects of a single act.

An extension of Fox's understanding of the simultaneity of the acts in the poem is a structuring idea in what follows. If the acts of the poem are all the same act, then the speech acts in the poem are all one, too. While this factor is not an organizing idea in her commentary, Fox does consider instances when two speeches must be identified with one another. Commenting on Milton's first and last final speeches in the poem, Fox observes the paradox of the poem is that the two speeches are identical:

> In Book I the poet was resolute, to be sure, but his speech was filled with questions: "O when Lord Jesus wilt thou come?" "What do I here before the Judgment? without my Emanation? / With the

> Daughters of Memory, & not with the Daughters of Inspiration [?]" (14:18, 28–29). Now he has learned the answers: Jesus will come when "Generation is swallowd up in Regeneration", which is the annihilation of the selfhood; descent into Generation is regeneration, is the prelude to Judgment, is the substitution of Inspiration for Memory; Ololon could have been here all along, had he only known to seek her here. The paradox of the poem is that the two speeches are identical, that the second is merely the manifestation in time of the first in eternity, that the answers are the asking of the questions. No time has elapsed between the speeches, for Milton entered Generation as he spoke the first and arrives in Generation as he speaks the second. The only difference between the two is the crucial difference of perspective which is, after all, the only difference between time and eternity. (1976: 176)

And she concludes that Ololon's two most important speeches are also identical.

> She has always asked the same thing: "how is this wondrous thing: / This World beneath, unseen before: this refuge from the wars / Of Great Eternity!" (21:47–49); "Is Ololon the cause of this?" (40:14). In eternity she cried, "Let us descend also, and let us give / Ourselves to death" (21:45–46); now she vows, "Thou goest to Eternal Death, and all must go with thee". Ololon's final speech here in Blake's garden is, like Milton's, a reflection of the first words she spoke, and the relationship between these two speeches is the same as that between Milton's: they are identical, the last speech simply the temporal manifestation of the Edenic situation in the first. The answer to her questions is the asking of them. The only difference is perspective, and now we see fully what a crucial difference that is. For Ololon's decision in Eden was a kind of parenthetical aside, a single plate among twenty-nine other plates that dealt with other things; but here in time, her decision is the crux of the poem's whole action, the trigger of apocalypse. It is only in time that the full extent of Ololon's failure is apparent, for time is ruled and ordered by such failure. Similarly, it is in time that reversal of that failure will have its profoundest effect, for that reversal will abolish time. (1976: 180-181)

But Fox's analysis stops well short of the notion that *all* speech acts in the poem are aspects of a single act, an idea which underpins the present commentary.

Argument and Structure

These sources not only provide some key insights, but also alert us to a lacuna in Blake studies, which this study addresses. What is suggested by the foregoing is a study of Blake's *Milton*, informed by Austin, which addresses Blake's poem and speech acts. To date, no one has produced such an analysis. Commentators working with Blake and language have failed to harness the insights of Esterhammer. Certainly, no critic has used her ideas in connection with Blake's *Milton*. Jones's *Blake on Language, Power, and Self-Annihilation* represents a Bakhtin-inspired investigation. It includes a chapter on *Milton*, which advances the argument that the crucial dynamic in the poem is the move away from monologism to dialogism (2010: 20). Cogan's *Blake and the Failure of Prophecy* is a Ricœur-informed discussion of Blake, which also includes a chapter on *Milton*. My own study is animated by a conviction that it is an Austin-inspired reading of *Milton* that is needed by Blake Studies.[7]

At the very end of this study, I will discuss Blake's *Milton* itself as a speech act. But this study is dedicated to speech acts on the part of characters in the poem. (This focus allows me to consider the Bard's Song, a significant part of the poem, as a speech act.) If we bear in mind the foregoing points – especially the fact that many of the speech acts in the poem belong to an instant, and that certain features of the poem's speech acts 'trouble' the idea of a moral dialectic – we can proceed to a simple iteration of the argument of this study: in *Milton*, sacred history is characterized by speech acts, and, ultimately, that history arrives at its conclusion by means of a specific group of such acts.

At times the commentary on a speech needs to be quite extended. The most expansive discussions of individual speech acts go through all three dimensions of the performative outlined by Austin: locution, illocution and perlocutionary effect. When writing this commentary in the idiom of speech act theory, it quickly became apparent that a light-touch is required in terms of the employment of the terminology. The repeated use of the full battery of terms characteristic of this approach can only make a commentary unappealingly lugubrious. Hence, the employment of the vocabulary in question is strategic.

Chapters 1 and 2 deal with the use of speech in the first structural part of Blake's poem, which is called the Bard's Song; chapter 2 partly deals with the Bard's Song as a speech act, the effect the Song has on Milton, and how he responds with a speech of his own. The Bard's Song deals with the Fall, and so here the speech acts are connected to developments associated with this early phase of Blake's myth, such as the emergence of Sin and Death as well as the creation of fallen space

14 *Introduction*

and time. That said, in Blake's mythology the story of the Fall is also the story of the *limits* to the Fall which also contains the seeds of restoration, so the developments and speech acts in this part are also auguries of apocalypse. After an initial contextual discussion, Chapter 1 deals first with Los's scolding Satan, Palamabron's attempt to boost morale in a speech to his servants, and Los's attempts to resolve the conflict through peace-making. It proceeds with a discussion of Los's attempt to draw a line under the events of the day ('a blank in Nature'), which proves ineffective. Next, it turns to the trial conducted by the 'Great Solemn Assembly' and focuses on the speech made by Satan (revealing his hand) when the verdict goes against him. It explains how the creation of fallen space follows on from Satan's defeat and his performative use of language.

Chapter 2 begins with a commentary on how questions are raised in the assembly about the rightness of the condemnation of Satan, and how they are answered. It then turns to how another character, Luetha, steps forth and makes a speech in which she takes full responsibility for the preceding calamitous events. It is explained how through language use fallen time and death come into existence. The focus then shifts to the speech delivered by Milton after he hears the Bard's Song. His speech is of such consequence and carries so much meaning that a comprehensive treatment of it is unavoidable. The commentary on his speech focuses on a particular schema employed by Blake, namely the one involving 'Spectre' and 'Emanation'. A full account of Blake's view of these aspects of self is provided. Also of relevance to Milton's speech are Milton's own Puritanism, the Deism of Blake's age and the war in Europe in Blake's time, too, and this commentary establishes the significance of and connections between each these as well.

Chapter 3 focuses on the responses of the zoas and others to Milton's journeying redeemed self, which is determined to proceed to Blake's Golgonooza. It first explains how Milton's personality gets disaggregated in the poem, and how his redeemed self emerges as the first protagonist in Book I. It then gives consideration to the speeches of Enitharmon, Orc and the Shadowy Female, as well as Rahab and Tirzah. In contrast to Urizen's physical engagement with Milton's redeemed self, these figures do things with words: specifically, they express their opposition to his progress to Golgonooza, or, in the case of Rahab and Tirzah, attempt to deepen his predicament by successfully converting him to a different mission.

Chapter 4 deals with the speeches made when the Los-Blake-Milton character complex arrives at Golgonooza. After an account of the process whereby these three figures merge into one and observations about the

Introduction 15

significance of this development, the chapter turns to, first, how Los's sons address him and how Los responds, and, second, how the sons of Luvah speak to Los and how he responds to them. The speeches of both Los's sons and the sons of Luvah possess illocutionary force, but Los does enough with words to defend Milton and Blake from any threat posed by characters who fear Milton's arrival in Golgonooza.

Chapter 5 begins with commentary on Ololon's announcing her decision to descend, and follows her descent through each of its stages (Eden, Beulah, Ulro, and Golgonooza/Felpham), providing analysis of the speech acts in this structural section of the poem.

Chapter 6, which provides a long commentary of the ending of the poem, proceeds to the great finale of the poem where Milton faces Satan as well as Ololon, who emerges as his emanation. The commentary focuses upon the last all-important speech acts in the poem, in which Milton, utterly transformed by the foregoing events, speaks his way to the brink of apocalypse. He first verbally triumphs over Satan, before, again through language, actuating a separation in Ololon, which catalyzes not just a new unity with his emanation proper, but the onset of the restoration of mankind.

In 'Coda: *Milton* as Speech Act', the poem is discussed as a speech act, which involves considerations of what impact the act may have on the reader, and what the implications of this are *vis-à-vis* enlightenment and the freeing of Orc.

How to Use this Book

There are two ways of reading this book: one for Blake scholars and one for those who wish to develop an initial comprehensive understanding of Blake's *Milton*. The following commentary is punctuated with five 'Context' sections. It will quickly become apparent that the main text assumes knowledge of matters such as the Fall and the zoas' role in it, the geography of Blake's Golgonooza and so on. These context sections provide the necessary information about these aspects of Blake's poem. Blake scholars may happily ignore these sections, but those without prior knowledge of *Milton* should read them carefully as they make their way through this short monograph.

Notes

1 All references to Blake's texts are to Erdman's standard edition.
2 In accordance with the current convention, I use the plate numbering of Essick and Viscomi throughout when discussing the designs.

3 Austin sets up an opposition between constative and performative utterances. Much of the time, we use language to simply say things (constative), but we also do things via the power of speech – this is what he calls performative language use. Standard examples of doing things with words include making a bet, the taking of marriage vows and declaring war. Austin also introduces a more sophisticated vocabulary for performative language, distinguishing first between locution and illocution. The former is the linguistic utterance, the latter is the force generated by the utterance when it is successful or felicitous – when the surrounding reality or conventions compliment the locution. Austin's theory is also sophisticated when it comes to the fact that, even though 'conventional powers' dictate the kind of illocutionary force produced by a locution, the response to that illocutionary force on the part of the addressee has a certain autonomy: to an extent the result of the force is unpredictable, making speech acts more interesting and more worthy of study. Austin calls this last dimension of the speech act the perlocutionary effect. Says Petry, 'A bet remains a bet even if the loser doesn't pay the winner; to welsh on a bet doesn't unmake it. If I promise to be on time, the illocutionary status of my promise is unaltered even if my perlocutionary behavior is to arrive several hours late. When the generalissimo felicitously suspends the constitution, it's suspended even if a perlocutionary uprising hangs the generalissimo. Although perlocutionary events can ignore or undo as well as affirm the things done by words, the words' illocutionary status is unaffected if the convention is observed when the words are spoken' (2016: 16).
4 Interestingly, Wittreich argues that, like Blake, the historical Milton was, in part, committed to 'mental fight' rather than literal warfare. Milton's pamphlets, as well as 'the symbolic reading of the sixth book of *Paradise Lost*' are testimony to how one side of his self was dedicated to purely intellectual conflict (1975: 240–242).
5 Needless to say, the opposite prejudice – reverse chronological snobbery – is to be avoided, too.
6 The present author delivered a paper on Blake's *Milton* at this memorable conference.
7 From the point of view of this study, Jones's point of departure leads him to misread Blake's *Milton*. Jones argues that it is not the case that Blake's poems dramatize the necessity of a voice of prophetic authority; rather, what emerges in Blake's prophecies is the necessity of more voices being included in conversations between characters. His line of argumentation reduces the illocutionary force and perlocutionary effects of speech to the production of more speech, which places an unjustifiable limit on both. Cogan's most significant contribution to our understanding of *Milton* involves her introduction of the concept of '*parousia*' (something I shall return to at the very end of this monograph), which might seem independent from her selecting Ricoeur as a theorist. How Ricoeur can help us understand *Milton* remains an underdeveloped feature of her commentary on the poem.

References

Blake, W. (1988), *The Complete Poetry and Prose of William Blake: Newly Revised Edition*, ed. D. V. Erdman, University of California Press: Berkeley.

Cogan, L. (2021), *Blake and the Failure of Prophecy*, Houndmills: Palgrave.
Damon, S.F. (1988), *A Blake Dictionary: The Ideas and Symbols of William Blake*, Hanover: University Press of New England.
Eaves, M. (2012), 'Afterword: The End? Remember Me!', in *Re-envisioning Blake*, eds. M. Crosby, T. Patenaude and A. Whitehead, Houndmills: Palgrave, 225–231.
Essick, R.N. (1989), *William Blake and the Language of Adam*, Oxford: Clarendon Press.
Essick, R., and J. Viscomi. (1993), *Milton: A Poem and the Final Illuminated Works, The Ghost of Abel, On Homer's Poetry, On Virgil's Laocoön*. By W. Blake, Princeton: William Blake Trust/Princeton University Press.
Esterhammer, A. (1994), *Creating States: Studies in the Performative Language of John Milton and William Blake*, Toronto: University of Toronto Press.
Fox, S. (1976), *Poetic Form in Blake's Milton*, Princeton: Princeton University Press.
Frye, N. (1990), *Words with Power: Being A Second Study of the Bible and Literature*, New York: A Harvest/HBJ Book.
James, D. (1977), *Written Within and Without: A Study of Blake's Milton*, Frankfurt: Peter Lang.
Jones, J.H. (2010), *Blake on Language, Power, and Self-Annihilation*, Houndmills: Palgrave.
Petry, S. (2016), *Speech Acts and Literary Theory*, London: Routledge.
Riede, D.G. (1991), *Oracles and Hierophants: Constructions of Romantic Authority*, Ithaca: Cornell University Press.
Williams. N. (ed.), (2006), *Palgrave Advances in William Blake Studies*, Houndmills: Palgrave.
Wittreich, J. (1975), *Angel of Apocalypse: Blake's Idea of Milton*, Wisconsin: University of Wisconsin.

1 The Bard's Song I: From the Beginning Until the Creation of Fallen Space

In literary studies, we sometimes speak of the *syuzhet* and the *fabula*, the account of events presented (which may feature anachrony or non-chronological presentation) and the events as they unfold in time. In Blake's poem, the *syuzhet* begins *in medias res*. Indeed, we are close to the end of Blake's sacred history at the start of the poem. We are introduced to Milton in Eternity, where he cuts an unhappy figure, and we are informed that he chooses to leave heaven.

Blake as narrator ('homodiegetic narrator' in Genette's vocabulary) immediately uses performative language: he issues a command aimed at the Daughters of Beulah, whom he has invoked, instructing them to explain what caused Milton to quit heaven after one hundred years of 'pondring the intricate mazes of Providence' (2.17, E96). The illocutionary force of his order registers, and having had his speech enabled by the Daughters, he answers his own question: on hearing the song of a Bard, Blake can now say, Milton realizes that he must return to the world again.

If the scale of an *analepsis* is judged by reach and extent, the Song is the ultimate *analepsis*: it tells us of everything that happens from the beginning of the Fall to the time when we encounter Milton in heaven as the instant before apocalypse occurs. Mainly, it is told through the story of Palamabron, Rintrah and Satan, as well as their father Los. In the process, the Song also explains aspects of fallen existence which Milton accounts for in *Paradise Lost*: we learn about Satan's fall, and of Satan's female companion, Luetha, who is identified as Sin, and of how she gives birth to Death. Other salient features of the Song include: a description of how pity and wrath become a dichotomy; accounts of the creation of fallen space and time; and an origins story dealing how the three classes of fallen humanity come to have their roles. Crucially, much of Milton's own vision will be corrected by the content of the Song.

DOI: 10.4324/9781003342571-2

The Bard's Song I 19

This chapter and the second chapter deal with the Bard's Song, and their main focus will be speech acts integral to the story of Los and his sons. But, in its first subsection, this chapter focuses on what happens *before* that time. The Bard's Song and some of the other material in Blake's poem provide an account of the earlier stages of the Fall, and we might profitably begin by turning to this material, which takes us all the way back to the beginning of Blake's *fabula*. As indicated by its subtitle, this chapter proceeds as far as the creation of fallen space.

The Earliest Stages of the Fall: Context I

Blake's representative of unfallen mankind is the very English titanic figure of Albion. Blake also thinks of the unfallen world in terms of a Jerusalem built on English soil, and he often speaks of Jerusalem as the bride or 'emanation' of Albion. For Blake, the Fall of mankind is an event primarily related to an Atlantic kingdom and the Jerusalem built there. As we shall see presently, he thinks of history in terms of cycles: the cycles connected to Asia and the period when scripture was written postdate a mythical Atlantic period. Blake also postulates that the writings of the Bible are based upon even more ancient holy texts, produced during the earlier cycles, an Atlantic cycle in particular. Atlantic scriptures, the first possible scriptures, Blake concludes, would have included a memory of the 'Jerusalem' built 'on England's green and pleasant land'. Clarifying that this is not a physical place but a spiritual one, and that myth should not be taken literally, Frye also calls this place a 'mental state' (2004: 361). As such, it is projected both into a distant past and the future in Blake's mythology. In 'And did those feet in ancient time', it is clear that the English Jerusalem is associated with both the pre-lapsarian world and a future achievement. In Blake's symbolism, Albion is identifiable with the celestial city, that city can also be thought of as 'Golgonooza', which mankind slowly builds in time, and Jerusalem is simultaneously the emanation of Albion and that city in its finished state. Frye talks us through these subtleties:

> The construction of character or identity out of life is part of the attempt of Albion to emerge from eternity as One Man who is also a City of God. Thus the imagination exists immortally not only as a person but as part of a growing and consolidating city, the Golgonooza which when complete will be the emanation or total achievement of Albion, Jerusalem. (Frye, 2004: 247)

Blake associates the pre-lapsarian Albion with 'zoas', a word derived from the Book of Revelation. (The author of Revelation, John of Patmos, speaks of a vision in which he sees 'four beasts ["zoa" (Gk. pl.)] full of eyes before and behind ... And the first beast was like a lion, and the second beast like a calf, and the third beast had a face as a man, and the fourth beast was like a flying eagle' (Revelation 4:6–7).) Their names are Urthona, Urizen, Tharmas and Luvah. Tharmas is located in the west, Urizen in the south, Luvah in the east and Urthona in the north. For Blake, the zoas were the four attributes of Albion, mankind as a fourfold male figure in the unfallen state.

In the post-lapsarian world, the zoas are 'Four Universes ... chaotic' (19.15, E112), and Albion or humanity is fallen or 'slain' or sleeping – resurrection will take the form of Albion waking up from slumbers. But the Fall also brings into existence fallen versions of the zoas. Urthona becomes a character called Los; Luvah becomes Orc; Urizen becomes Satan; and Tharmas the Covering Cherub. Moreover, in the Fall, male and female become separated from one another, as well, and so every fallen zoa has a female counterpart. Thus, when Urthona becomes Los, he splits from Enitharmon, his emanation; Luvah, becoming Orc, splits from his female counterpart, Vala; Urizen separates from Ahania; and the fall of Tharmas releases his emanation, Enion. As well as eternal and temporal manifestations, the zoas also have spectral selves. As Blake proceeded, more and more spectre figures became integral to his vision.

To turn more specifically to *Milton*, along with their unfallen manifestations, the fallen zoas are central to what happens in the poem. We learn of the moment when Orc comes into existence and also of how Satan is 'brought forth' by Enitharmon. As regards emanations, in *Milton* it is only Jerusalem, Albion's emanation, Enthitharmon, Los's emanation, and the Shadowy Female, the fallen version of Luvah's emanation, Vala, in additional to Milton's own emanation, who are important, though, as we shall see, other emanations get referred to. Spectral figures are also important in *Milton*. Los, Albion, Satan, Luvah, and Orc all have spectres, and Satan is identified as Milton's own spectre (though Satan is also identified as 'the Spectre of Albion', and it is said that he has his own spectre, too).

Both *The Four Zoas* and *Jerusalem* provide elaborate variations on the theme of the beginning of sacred history (the *fabula* beginning). In *Milton*, Blake uses an astonishing shorthand when referencing the start of the Fall. It is of the greatest importance that the zoas stick to their positions and roles. We can see the zoas in their eternal positions in the design of plate 32. On one level, the Fall begins when Luvah moves from his eastern realm to Urizen's in the south, where he seizes Urizen's chariot of light, an episode which, like Satan's taking control of the Harrow, reminds us of the story in which Ovid's Phaethon commandeers the chariot of his father. In Blake's other epics, this is one episode out of several; in *Milton*, the early part of the Fall is reduced to this development:

> Four Universes round the Mundane Egg remain Chaotic
> One to the North, named Urthona: One to the South, named Urizen:
> One to the East, named Luvah: One to the West, named Tharmas
> They are the Four Zoas that stood around the Throne Divine!
> But when Luvah assum'd the World of Urizen to the South:
> And Albion was slain upon his mountains, & in his tent;
> All fell towards the Center in dire ruin, sinking down.
> And in the South remains a burning fire; in the East a void.
> In the West, a world of raging waters; in the North a solid,
> Unfathomable! without end. (19.15–24, E112–113)

Like each of the zoas, Tharmas is connected to a sense and an element, in addition to a compass point. As well as the west, he is the water that overwhelms the land ('a world of raging water'). In *The Four Zoas*, the Fall proceeds with a deluge, which reduces the Atlantic kingdom to an archipelago (Britain and Ireland) hemmed in by 'the Sea of Time and Space' (the Atlantic ocean) or behind a 'Gate' to the west. Tharmas is also the sense of taste, and this explains why in *The Four Zoas* the Fall is spoken of as the moment when the 'Gate of the Tongue' was closed, and why in *Milton* we are told of how 'the Nerves of the Tongue are closed' (29.40, E128).

This aspect of the fallen state also places limits on human creativity. Of relevance are the two heavens of Blake's cosmos: the higher, superior heaven, Eden, and the lower but still paradisal realm of Beulah, the fourfold and threefold worlds. Beulah lies immediately below Eden, although the inhabitants see it otherwise (30.8–14, E129). Speaking of a ladder of creativity, Frye states that

> The material world is in a way feminine to the perceiver; it is the body which receives the seed of his imagination, and the works of the imagination which are the artist's children are drawn from that body. ... But as the artist develops, he becomes more and more interested in the art and more and more impatient of the help he receives from nature. In the world of Eden there is only energy

incorporating itself in form, creator and creature, which means that somewhere (on the upper limit of Beulah, as it happens) this permanent objective body which nourishes and incubates the imaginative drops out. (2004: 81)

Frye suggests that for as long as the 'Western Gate' remains closed, there will be a division between human and divine power, meaning that the creativity of the state of Eden or fourfold world is unobtainable for the artist. 'Even for the visionary who lives in the divine Paradise in which creation and perception are the same thing', observes Frye, 'the gulf between Pygmalion's human power and the divine power that brought it to life still exists' (2004: 277). Indeed, under such conditions, the art *and* love of artist will forever be subject painful limitations. The artist cannot bring his or her art to life; additionally, experience confirms that the beloved, like the child, is not simply a 'creature of the imagination'. 'The barrier between art and love', Frye tells us, 'is part of the closed Western Gate', which will remain closed until 'the final apocalypse, when the Creator twisting the sinews of the tiger's heart will also be producing a work of art, a beloved object, and a child of his imagination all at once' (ibid.).

*

Interestingly, we are provided with the above potted version of this phase of sacred history (19.15–24, E112–113) half-way through Book I, *after* the Bard's Song, at a relatively advanced stage of the *syuzhet*. The Bard provides snapshots of the Fall early in his song, but he speeds through his narrative, stopping only to furnish us with more detail when he gets to Urizen and Los, who is central to his song.

As in the earlier *The Four Zoas*, in *Milton* all hopes rest on Los, the fallen Urthona. In the earlier poem, the first books carefully plot the demise (the fall) of the other zoas, leaving Los as the last hope; in *Milton*, the backdrop is less clear, but Los is unequivocally at the centre of the action. 'Urizen lay in darkness & solitude, in chains of the mind lock'd up' (3.6, E96), recounts the Bard. The emphasis is first on Los's efforts to give Urizen a human form over the course of seven ages. (The sequence is familiar to readers of *The Four Zoas*, and was first presented by Blake in *The (First) Book of Urizen*.) The emphasis then shifts to Los himself. In time, a male and female forms separate themselves from him: his emanation, Enitharmon, and Los's Spectre, the Spectre of Urthona.

Making his spectre work for him, Los builds Generation and Golgonooza. In *Milton*, Generation will be counterpoised with

'Regeneration'. Religious thought stresses the different between creation and generation. Christ is generated not created, we learn: the point is that Christ is consubstantial with God. In *Milton*, generation has the same significance. It is only at this point that something along the lines of reproduction comes into sacred history. And the story proceeds with a series of important births, already alluded to: Orc and the Shadowy Female as well as Los's sons. Satan, the last of Los's sons, also enters the action at this stage. For now, of course, Los and Enitharmon are oblivious to the fact that Satan is Urizen in Generation.

The England and the world which emerges is one dominated by what Blake calls Druidism, which Frye describes as 'a cult of death consisting largely of human sacrifices' (2004: 132). (A Druid trilithon dominates the design of plate 4.) Druidism is to spread through time and place: in time, it covers the globe, and it is still a force in Blake's day. The Bard speaks of how it is Druidism that supplants the English Jerusalem and spreads to the four corners of the world – and how it will endure until Jerusalem is built once again:

> Loud sounds the Hammer of Los, & loud his Bellows is heard
> Before London to Hampsteads breadths & Highgates heights To Stratford & old Bow: & across to the Gardens of Kensington
> On Tyburns Brook: loud groans Thames beneath the iron Forge
> Of Rintrah & Palamabron of Theotorm & Bromion, to forge the instruments
> Of Harvest: the Plow & Harrow to pass over the Nations
>
> The Surrey hills glow like the clinkers of the furnace: Lambeths Vale
> Where Jerusalems foundations began; where they were laid in ruins
> Where they were laid in ruins from every Nation & Oak Groves rooted
> Dark gleams before the Furnace-mouth a heap of burning ashes
> When shall Jerusalem return & overspread all the Nations
> Return: return to Lambeths Vale O building of human souls
> Thence stony Druid Temples overspread the Island white
> And thence from Jerusalems ruins.. from her walls of salvation
> And praise: thro the whole Earth were reard from Ireland
> To Mexico & Peru west, & east to China & Japan; till Babel
> The Spectre of Albion frownd over the Nations in glory & war
> All things begin & end in Albions ancient Druid rocky shore

> But now the Starry Heavens are fled from the mighty limbs of Albion
>
> Loud sounds the Hammer of Los, loud turn the Wheels of Enitharmon
> Her Looms vibrate with soft affections, weaving the Web of Life
> Out from the ashes of the Dead; Los lifts his iron Ladles
> With molten ore: he heaves the iron cliffs in his rattling chains
> From Hyde Park to the Alms-houses of Mile-end & old Bow.
> (6.1–31, E99–100)

As Summerfield explains:

> The primeval Jerusalem that covered the earth has been ruined and replaced by Druid oak groves and temples, while the nations have been set at odds and reduced to a state of continual war. The corrupt druidic religion prescribing human sacrifice for moral trespass also claims innumerable victims ranging from those slain on Aztec and Inca alters to executed criminals and Jesus crucified – Blake equates Calvary and the site of Tyburn gallows. (1998: 233)

The reader will notice that Urizen is given form by Los 'among indefinite Druid rocks & snows of doubt& reasoning' (3.8, E97). Howard argues that by situating Urizen's construction in among the Druid rocks, 'Blake connects the moralistic sacrificial nature of Druidism with rationalism' (1976: 95). And he associates mathematics with Druidism as well. Having clarified how Blake found 'the Druidic universe of mathematics' in the work of Thomas Paine, Howard suggests that 'The mathematical proportion [5.44, E99] of the Druid, and its snowy reasoning, is Blake's symbol for the "mathematical science" whose principles underlie the "vast machinery" of the Deistic, Newtonion universe' (1976: 97).

Trouble in the Threefold World

The story of Los and his sons is an account of later stages of the Fall, and it includes a number of speech acts which fail to forestall the continuation of the Fall. At the same time, certain speech acts which contribute to that continuation will, paradoxically, have a providential character. Although Blake is largely concerned with the Fall, that event in his mythology is not without a sense of anticipated restoration. When speaking of Aristotle's concept of *anagnorisis*, Frye says 'If a plot begins and ends, the beginning must somehow suggest an end, and the end return to the beginning', and this is true of *Milton*. Hence, the speeches of the Bard's Song also suggest the ultimate restoration of things in resurrection and apocalypse.

Los and his three sons – Palamabron, Rintrah and Satan – live a symbolically agricultural existence, although, at the same time, Los retains his identity as a smith, which he always has in Blake's poetry. Los's eldest son, Rintrah, is responsible for the Plow; Palamabron, his second son, controls the Harrow; Satan toils in the Mills referred to in 'Jerusalem', with which *Milton* begins. The three characters belong to different 'classes', namely the Elect (Satan), the Reprobate (Rintrah) and the Redeemed (Palamabron).

'The three classes belong to the sexual threefold world of Beulah, not the human fourfold world of Eden, and hence are involved in the fallen world' (2005a: 261), states Frye, which means that conflict spells trouble. In the song everything descends from Satan and Palamabron's switching roles, whereby Satan takes over the use of the Harrow. The speeches begin at this stage, too, and we may now turn exclusively to speech acts. At first the emphasis is on speech acts which deepen the Fall. Certain speech acts, such as those of Los, as we shall see, aim to forestall this negative development but prove ineffective.

At first, Satan is a harmless-seeming and persuasive figure. Work with the Harrow exhausts Palamabron, and Satan, in a solicitous manner, offers to relieve his brother. The Bard does not share Satan's initial speech with us, but it is clear that it does not have the perlocutionary effect Satan wanted. The exchange, we learn, turns agonistic. In a reprimand, which needs to be followed up by a second locution, Los refuses Satan's request in no uncertain terms. Before the second, more ill-tempered reprimand, mixing the metaphor of the mill with that of the loom, he reminds Satan of his role, which Los feels Satan should be grateful for: as 'Newtons Pantocrator' ('pantocrator' is a term coined by Newton), Satan is in charge of the production of material reality, metaphorically a woven fabric, 'the Woof of Locke', associated with the Englishman because of his materialist philosophy. (We shall return to this connection between Newton and Locke.) Satan's task *is* a lowly one, especially when compared to that of Palamabron, but Los seems genuine in his reaction, the power of his language deriving partly from the fact that he is a *pater familias* figure:

> If you account it Wisdom when you are angry to be silent, and
> Not to shew it: I do not account that Wisdom but Folly.
> Every Mans Wisdom is peculiar to his own Individualty
> O Satan my youngest born, art thou not Prince of the Starry Hosts
> And of the Wheels of Heaven, to turn the Mills day & night?

> Art thou not Newtons Pantocrator weaving the Woof of Locke
> To Mortals thy Mills seem every thing & the Harrow of Shaddai
> A scheme of Human conduct invisible & incomprehensible
> Get to thy Labours at the Mills & leave me to my wrath.
>
> Satan was going to reply, but Los roll'd his loud thunders.
>
> Anger me not! thou canst not drive the Harrow in pitys paths.
> Thy Work is Eternal Death, with Mills & Ovens & Cauldrons.
> Trouble me no more. thou canst not have Eternal Life.
> (4.6–14, E98)

Los's speech fails to produce the perlocutionary effect he hoped for: Satan, his wayward son, is not cowed by it and trouble continues to brew.

Ultimately, Satan's solicitations pay off. We are not provided with Satan's exact words, but they are certainly performatives which fly in the face of the socio-political order, structured around family, the division of labour and a kind of class system. The perlocutionary effect is represented by Los's reaction to Satan's speech: taken in by Satan's 'endearing love', Los gives Palamabron's station to Satan for a day. Importantly and wrongly, Palamabron does not verbally demur – he fears Los will side with Satan and conclude that he, Palamabron, is an ingrate. The continuation of the Fall, then, is first eventuated by Los's mistake and Palamabron's bad judgement in the wake of Satan's success with words.

At the close of day, Palamabron finds 'the horses of the harrow/ ... maddend with tormenting fury' (7.17–18, E100), owing to Satan's tenure of the Harrow. Of course he responds by making the next important speech of the Song. In terms of his intention, he wishes to calm the nerves of his servants: he assures them of Satan's ultimate defeat and even suggests that if he speaks to Los, the evolving crisis may be averted. He is quick to remind his audience that the avoidance of revenge is a moral imperative. Later, many of the Eternals who listen to the Song comment 'Pity and Love are too venerable for the imputation/ Of Guilt' (13.48, E107), but Palamabron can separate emotional wheat from chaff and is therefore clear-eyed about the phoniness of Satan's bogus 'pity and love'. He also acknowledges his mistake in not objecting to Los's proposal. His reticence was a mistake; the situation called for a powerful (no doubt performative) speech act:

> You know Satans mildness and his self-imposition,
> Seeming a brother, being a tyrant, even thinking himself a brother
> While he is murdering the just; prophetic I behold
> His future course thro' darkness and despair to eternal death

> But we must not be tyrants also! he hath assum'd my place
> For one whole day, under pretence of pity and love to me:
> My horses hath he madden! and my fellow servants injur'd:
> How should he know the duties of another? O foolish forbearance
> Would I had told Los, all my heart! but patience O my friends.
> All may be well: silent remain, while I call Los and Satan.
> (7.21–30, E100–101)

In a speech which is only alluded to, Palamabron then informs Los of the disorder Satan has caused. Unbowed, Satan plays the part of the victim. Los, half-taken in, uses speech to separate the two as though separating squabbling children:

> Henceforth Palamabron, let each his own station
> Keep: nor in pity false, nor in officious brotherhood, where
> None needs, be active. (7.41–43, E101)

As Rieger observes, it is deeply ironical that Palamabron should be scolded thus by Los: it is Satan who is faking it (1973: 265). Despite Los's socio-political standing, this order ultimately proves ineffective as well. Palamabron finds that, whatever success his speech enjoyed, the creatures of the Harrow are still in disarray, and, while he is trying to curb the disorder, Satan continues his verbal manipulation of Los (8.1–3, E101). Satan then returns to the mills, only to find that Palamabron's time at the mills has resulted in a comparable chaos (8.4–7, E101). 'The Angel', observes Frye, 'cannot feel the honest indignation which is the voice of God: he may simulate it to the point of deceiving himself, but there will always be a concealed selfish reason for expressing it' (2004: 75). Frye's description reminds us of Satan of course: he conducts himself in the manner of a Blakean Angel. Convinced he is the injured party, Satan, heightening the tension through bitter complaint, again speaks to Los of his unhappiness – again, the speech is only alluded to. Los visits the Mills, where he sees for himself 'The servants of the Mills drunken with wine and dancing wild' (8.8, E101).

Los's verbal interventions have failed to forestall the developing crisis. Now he attempts to bring the unhappiness to an end by a rallying performative use of language directed at those who labour for Satan at the mills. He instructs them, first, to follow him, and, second, to resume their work on the following day. He also performatively blames himself for the evolving crisis, identifying feelings of pity as the prime mover. As Rieger suggests, in the poem, pity, like wrath, is 'an epidemic throughout Eden' (1973: 266):

> Ye Genii of the Mills! the Sun is on high
> Your labours call you! Palamabron is also in sad dilemma;
> His horses are mad! his Harrow confounded! his companions enrag'd.
> Mine is the fault! I should have remember'd that pity divides the soul
> And man, unmans: follow with me my Plow. this mournful day
> Must be a blank in Nature: follow with me, and tomorrow again
> Resume your labours, & this day shall be a mournful day.
> (8.16–22, E102)

(Later in the poem, Rintrah and Palamabron will offer resistance to Los, accusing him of feeling pity for 'evil' (23: 18–20, E118).)

This performative fails as well. Los has tried to take charge of the situation, but it becomes apparent that events have slipped out of his control. A larger conflict starts to break out. Other figures in this world – the other sons of Los but also the archangel Michael – start to side with either Satan or Palamabron (8.29–33, E102). Of great significance, as we shall see, is that Rintrah is enormously partisan:

> But Rintrah who is of the reprobate: of those form'd to destruction
> In Indignation. for Satans soft dissimulation of friendship!
> Flam'd above all the plowed furrows, angry red and furious.
> (8.34–36, E102)

The threefold world, we might say, is in free-fall. Satan's use of language and his actions are key to the developments, but, more importantly, the developments are the result of the *ineffectiveness* of the Los's (sociopolitical) performative speech. Jones argues that 'progress' is always towards dialogue and more inclusive exchanges, but it is difficult to argue that that kind of communication is the ideal illustrated by Satan's exchanges with Los about his taking charge of the Harrow. Here an exchange of views ultimately leads to a deepening of the Fall.

Satan and Fallen Space

In the next significant development, Palamabron resolves to turn to a jury, 'a Great Solemn Assembly' (8.46, E102), in the hope that its verdict may go in his favour. Rintrah and Palamabron rise as witnesses, but something surprising happens, although it is less surprising if we bear in mind that on plate 8, when Blake is describing the conflict of the day before, Satan is described as being thoroughly Rintrah-like in his wrath: as Rieger points out, both characters are described with the adjectives 'red' and 'angry' (8.36–38, E102). We are informed that when the performative pronouncing of a verdict (the judgement) was received, 'it fell on Rintrah and his rage:/ Which now flam'd high & furious *in* Satan against Palamabron' (9.10–11, E103, my emphasis). (Sutherland suggests that the influence of Rintrah on Satan is visualized in the full-page design on plate 8: Rintrah's left foot is making contact with Satan's right, the former's anger being channelled to Satan in this way (1977: 151).) On plate 9, we learn that this means that Satan is not be condemned. But, as we shall see, he is identified as the guilty party on plate 11. The only way to understand what happens next is to assume that Satan *understands* he is viewed as the guilty party, even if the judgement does not fall (directly) on him. Like Milton's own Satan, who 'thought himself impair'd' (5.665), Blake's Satan suffers from a kind of pathological victimhood, and his sense of injustice is exacerbated by this turn of events. Incensed, he accuses Palamabron of ingratitude, while still 'flaming with Rintrahs fury hidden beneath his own mildness' (9.19, E103), the perlocutionary effect of the verdict beginning to register. Giving in to his rage, he creates the Seven Deadly Sins to 'pervert the Divine voice in its entrance to earth' (9.23, E103), along with laws and punishments. Then, his mask falling, he reveals his true self in a wholly unguarded speech – an agonistic performative statement demanding obedience which serves to reveal the megalomaniac self birthed in his hothouse imagined oppression. Blake was unconvinced by Milton's portrayal of Satan and the Messiah. Now Blake's version of Milton's Satan declares himself God:

... I am God alone
There is no other! let all obey my principles of moral individuality
I have brought them from the uppermost innermost recesses
Of my Eternal Mind, transgressors I will rend off for ever,
As now I rend this accursed Family from my covering. (9.25–29, E103)

'Satan', observes James, 'being both usurper and oppressor, mimics both Milton's God and his Satan' (1977: 30).

Perlocutionary effects ripple out from Satan's declaration. In one respect, his speech is an unsuccessful performative, carrying no illocutionary force. Success, after all, would depend on his addressees accepting that he is God and therefore worthy of obedience, but they don't and therefore he has no such power. But his speech nonetheless actually proves to be a phenomenological performative of enormous import, altering the reality of the universe around him.

Eden and Beulah date from the earliest ages of the Blake's universe; Generation comes into existence at a later time, as we have seen. As Satan's rage intensifies, another location, Ulro, the creation of which seems connected to his verbal apoplexy, appears in the depths of his being:

> Thus Satan rag'd amidst the Assembly! and his bosom grew
> Opake against the Divine Vision: the paved terraces of
> His bosom inwards shone with fires, but the stones becoming opake!
> Hid him from sight, in an extreme blackness and darkness,
> And there a World of deeper Ulro was open'd, in the midst
> Of the Assembly. In Satans bosom a vast unfathomable Abyss.
> (9:30–35, E103)

We are then told of another speech act: Satan reprimands the Divine Mercy 'for protecting Palamabron in his tent' (9.42, E103). Rintrah reacts to Satan's continued aggressive bearing towards Palamabron and separates the two with columns of fire, but Satan immediately destroys them, which has implications for the two emotions which have dominated the action from the start: pity and wrath. If we may postpone our consideration of this development in order to retain a focus on 'space', we then learn of how Satan sinks down 'a dreadful Death' (9.48, E103) and of how his spectre descends 'into its Space' (9.52, E104). This is not something Satan does through speech. But it is the beginning of a culmination of developments that speech has been central to.

The important revelation about this space is positioned slightly earlier. Immediately prior to the trial, Enitharmon creates a protective space for Satan and the archangel Michael when conflict involving all of Los's sons erupts: 'She form'd a Space for Satan & Michael & for the poor infected' (8.43, E102). It seems to be this space which Satan's spectre descends to. Enitharmon was unaware of Satan's other identity when she created the space of course. She and Los now understand that Satan is the form Urizen takes when Orc and the Shadowy Female drag him down into the world of Generation (10.1, E104). Enitharmon, we are told, often enters the space weeping – Blake provides an image of her in the design of plate 8*(c). The space is subsequently characterized as a 'Female Space' (10.6, E104): in the chapter after this one, we'll turn to Blake's conception of the Female Will. Satan then causes the space to fall. The space has been identified as Canaan, but then we are told that it is identifiable as Canaan as a result of its fall:

> And Satan vibrated in the immensity of the Space! Limited
> To those without but Infinite to those within: it fell down and
> Became Canaan. (10.8–10, E104)

The spaces are ultimately the same place, Canaan and Ulro being alternate terms for the lowest regions of universe in Blake's vocabulary. Ulro is to Eden what Canaan is to the Promised Land; hence, there is obviously a close connection between this Canaan and the Ulro which appeared in Satan's bosom. England is not mentioned, but just as 'Atlantis, Eden, and the Promised Land are the same place' (Frye, 2005a: 308), so such a space in Blake will always be suggestive of not just Ulro and Canaan but also England, the fallen Atlantic kingdom. In other words, much of what we recognize as our world is brought into existence by the foregoing, unequivocally phenomenological, speech acts. The last we hear of Satan (for now) is represented by a description of him imitating God from his seat in 'Albions ancient Druid rocky shore' (6.25, E100):

> And the Mills of Satan were separated into a moony Space
> Among the rocks of Albions Temples, and Satans Druid sons
> Offer the Human Victims throughout all the Earth, and Albions
> Dread Tomb immortal on his Rock, overshadowd the whole Earth:
> Where Satan making to himself Laws from his own identity.
> Compell'd others to serve him in moral gratitude & submission
> Being call'd God: setting himself above all that is called God.
> And all the Spectres of the Dead calling themselves Sons of God
> In his Synagogues worship Satan under the Unutterable Name.
> (11.6–14, E104)

Pity and Wrath Rent Asunder

This part of the Bard's Song is also the story of pith and wrath. (Blake may also have inscribed the two emotions in the design of the poem. Rix suggests that the tiny warrior and shepherd figures discernible in the design of plate 4 represent wrath and pity, respectively (1984: 110).) To return to the speech act I alluded to a moment ago, in a fit of pique Satan denounces the Divine Family for protecting Palamabron. It is Rintrah who reacts, he who provides the perlocutionary effect:

> Rintrah rear'd up walls of rocks and pourd rivers & moats
> Of fire round the walls: columns of fire guard around
> Between Satan and Palamabron in the terrible darkness. (9.43–45, E103)

It might appear as though Rintrah is simply protecting Palamabron from Satan's fury, but when Satan destroys Rintrah's walls, it becomes clear that Rintrah's act has implications for the relations between pity and wrath:

> And Satan not having the Science of Wrath, but only of Pity:
> Rent them asunder, and wrath was left to wrath, & pity to pity. (9. 47–47, E103)

We may draw the inference that in response to Satan's bluster, Rintrah tries to unite pity and wrath.

Pity is suggestive of a kind of *coinvolvement* with the world. Wrath is its opposite. Interestingly, Blake himself has both 'sciences'. As Frye has persuasively argued, Blake, as a visionary in the fallen world of the early nineteenth century, 'has two sciences, the science of wrath and the science of pity' (2004: 103). 'This contrast', Frye continues, 'Blake calls Rintrah and Palamabron, both of whom are different aspects of himself' (ibid.). But, predominantly, the two sciences are distinct in fallen life. And Blake is interested in dramatizing the opposition not just through Rintrah and Palamabron, but also through Rintrah and Satan. It is as though Satan and Rintrah are the guiding spirits of fallen life in this regard. Satan does not have the 'science of Wrath'; Rintrah is a stranger to the science of pity. By itself the science of wrath leaves humanity to its devices. It is likely that pity without wrath is the greater problem in the fallen world, however. Howard describes the results of that side of the dichotomy, where pity operates without wrath, in compelling terms:

> To have pity for suffering and not have wrath against the cause of suffering, whether the cause is another man, or ultimately a God, is, essentially, to accept the state of suffering as an inevitable condition. A reformer or a revolutionary cannot act without the

implication that he feels wrath against the cause of suffering as well as pity for the sufferer; but a bishop who preaches unmurmuring acceptance of an unfair earthly lot, a governmental apologist who allows no suggestion of change or hint that anything is wrong. They have no wrath. Satan's pity is the kind of pity that weeps for suffering but refuses to alleviate it. It is, in fact, the pity felt by the keeper of the status quo, who pities the suffering that he himself inflicts to protect himself. (1976: 78)

In response to Satan's words, Rintrah tries to heal the division between the two, but he is unsuccessful. Consequently, this feature of our post-lapsarian world also falls into place at this point, just as fallen space is coming into existence, but before fallen time and death become realities.

References

Blake, W. (1988), *The Complete Poetry and Prose of William Blake: Newly Revised Edition*, ed. D. V. Erdman, University of California Press: Berkeley.

Frye, N. (2004), *Fearful Symmetry: A Study of William Blake*, ed. N. Halmi, Toronto: University of Toronto Press.

Frye, N. (2005a), *Northrop Frye on Milton and Blake*, ed. A. Esterhammer, Toronto: University of Toronto Press.

Howard, J. (1976), *Blake's Milton: A Study in Selfhood*, London: Associated University Presses.

James, D. (1977), *Written Within and Without: A Study of Blake's Milton*, Frankfurt: Peter Lang.

Jones, J.H. (2010), *Blake on Language, Power, and Self-Annihilation*, Houndmills: Palgrave.

Rieger, J. (1973), '"The Hem of Their Garments": The Bard's Song in *Milton*', in *Blake's Sublime Allegory*, Madison: University of Wisconsin, 259–280.

Rix, D.S. (1984), '*Milton*: Blake's Reading of the Second Isaiah', in *Poetic Prophecy in Western Literature*, ed. J. Wojcik and R. Frontain, London: Associated University Press, 106–118.

Summerfield, H. (1998), *A Guide to the Books of William Blake for Innocent and Experienced Readers*, Gerrards Cross: Colin Smythe.

Sutherland, J.H. (1977), 'Blake's *Milton*: The Bard's Song', CLQ, XIII, 142–157.

2 The Bard's Song II: The Creation of Fallen Time and Death, and Milton's Response to the Song

Even if much of what we recognize as our world is brought into existence by the foregoing speech acts, we are only half-way through this mythical account of the origins of our world. The story of the three classes is complete (although a speaker is about to provide a commentary on it), but a number of important aspects of the fallen world have not yet come into existence: fallen time and death, specifically. In addition, 'sin' remains unidentified. The remainder of the Song deals with these issues.

As things progress, speech remains centre stage. An unidentified figure, whose question is reported, asks the Great Solemn Assembly why the innocent (Rintrah) should be condemned for the guilty (Satan). The response serves to shed light on the nature on the new reality created by the foregoing (speech) events; it also enlightens those listening. Thus far speech has apparently only served to deepen the Fall, making restoration an even more distant goal, but now we start to learn about how something restorative is also at work. The question is answered in short order: the guilty party cannot face condemnation as it would set off an unending cycle of sacrifices. We get a sense that the world which comes into existence here is not an inverted tyranny: it is something better. Additionally, it is not only that Satan as the guilty party cannot face 'Eternal Death' – it is also that he is unredeemable, and, for that reason, in the language of the poem, his class 'must be new Created continually moment by moment'. Of course the consequence of this is that, in fallen life, Satan and those of the Elect will represent a powerful class: later in Book I, Los will speak of how Satan *subdued* those of the other classes in this ancient setting. The three characters class associations are presented as a revelation. Palamabron and by extension the whole class of the redeemed belong to that class not just because they are redeemable, but also because Palamabron was 'redeem'd from Satans Law,

DOI: 10.4324/9781003342571-3

the wrath falling on Rintrah' (11.23, E104). (It is suggested that Palamabron, rather cannily, waited till Satan lost his temper before calling down the assembly.) In a sociopolitical performative, the speaker, clearly invested with the power to name and thereby identify, sums up the nature of the universal development:

> And it was enquir'd: Why in a Great Solemn Assembly
> The Innocent should be condemn'd for the Guilty? Then an Eternal rose
>
> Saying. If the Guilty should be condemn'd, he must be an Eternal Death
> And one must die for another throughout all Eternity.
> Satan is fall'n from his station & never can be redeem'd
> But must be new created continually moment by moment
> And therefore the Class of Satan shall be calld the Elect, & those
> Of Rintrah. the Reprobate, & those of Palamabron the Redeem'd
> For he is redeem'd from Satans Law, the wrath falling on Rintrah,
> And therefore Palamabron dared not to call a solemn Assembly
> Till Satan had assum'd Rintrahs wrath in the day of mourning
> In a feminine delusion of false pride self-deciev'd. (11.15–26, E105)

The conventional social classes are physical; Blake's classes are spiritual. This system consists of 'Reprobate,' 'Redeemed' and 'Elect'. Inverting Milton's moral categories, where the Elect are the moral, the Reprobate the damned, and the Redeemed are between the two, unsure of their own salvation, Blake, keeping the redeemed in the middle position, argues that the Reprobate are the saviours, and the Elect the contemptible. The Reprobate consists of those who possess extraordinary imaginative powers but are usually shunned by society. The Elect are those reactionary minds who are complicit in the continuation of all social evils, and for this reason they are the villains of this world. (Bloom suggests that, along with Milton himself, the historical figures referred to in the poem can be understood in relation to this schema: Milton is reprobate, Cromwell redeemed and Charles and James Elect (1982: 912).) Blake's conception of the three classes is partly an attempt to provide a framework for the fact that ours is a world in which innocent figures such as Christ and John the Baptist are punished, while the culpable, the Elect, enjoy rewards.

Luetha (Sin), Time and Death

Death

The Bard's Song comprises a twofold revelation about Satan. We have already considered the first of these, Satan's sudden revealing of his true nature after the verdict doesn't go his way. The second now ensues, and it comes by means of another speech. Like the epic poem it forms a part of, the Bard's Song actually begins *in medias res*. The song also tells us about the *original* catalyst of these developments, the real 'evil hour' as it were, and next it goes back to that moment. Greater powers are concealed by the figure of Satan: specifically, Luetha, who is identifiable with Sin. In *Paradise Lost*, Satan couples with Sin to produce Death after he has achieved his Satanic self. In the Bard's Song, Sin is identified as a prime mover is Satan's bid for power, which, as we shall see, in turn, results in the generation of Death.

The above pronouncement by the Eternal has another important effect: it precipitates a verbal intervention from Luetha. Presently, we'll turn to the effect of her speech act – the end section of the Bard's Song amounts to a fairly elaborate sequence of perlocutionary effects, but first we must consider the content of her intervention, paying special attention to her account of earlier speech acts.

Luetha informs the assembly of an earlier conflict between her and Elynittria, Palamabron's companion. Just as it is strongly felt emotion which actuates Satan, so Luetha is moved by love: 'I loved Palamabron', she declares. Luetha, we learn, approached Palamabron's tent, no doubt hoping to take the place of Elynittria and assist Palamabron with his horses, only to be repelled by the jealous Elynittria's arrows. Unbowed, she hatches a second plan. She extinguishes Satan 'masculine perceptions' (12.5, E105), thus engendering his 'soft/ Delusory love to Palamabron' (12.6–7, E105) (which seems to amount to 'admiration join'd with envy'), and his love for Palamabron fires him with a desire to commandeer Palamabron's work. In this way, Luetha calculated, she, as Satan's companion, would be able to do Elynittria's work.

Luetha then provides a first-hand account of Satan's unsuccessful driving of the harrow, which deepens our understanding of what transpired. Importantly, we learn different speech acts were instrumental in the earlier stages of Fall, although it is reported speech she provides. (Of course the narrative layers are manifold by this stage: in Luetha's direct speech, she reports her own earlier speech, as well as the earlier speech of Elynittria and Satan; her speech is an integral part of the Bard's Song, which comprises the direct speech of the Bard; and of course the Blakean narrator of the poem provides the Bard's Song, which, in turn, is provided by the Daughters of Beulah.) The performative speech acts begin with a plea and an exhortation: Luetha explains that when at noon Palamabron's horses issued a plea 'for rest and pleasant death', Luetha, impersonating Elynittria, emerged from Satan's breast, seeking to spur the steeds on. But the horses knew she was not Elynittria and responded in a frenzied manner. (Luetha describes herself as 'a bow/ Of varying colours': see the image of the rainbow in the design of plate 9.) Satan, trying to control the situation, ordered the gnomes (Palamabron's friends) to try to 'to curb the hoses', which they attempted to, but to no avail. The ensuing chaos reminds us of the damage wrought by Ovid's Phaethon, but here it is Albion and Jerusalem who are affected. The Gnomes turning on Satan, Luetha concealed herself inside Satan's brain. But when they refused to continue their labour, Luetha emerged from Satan's forehead to confront them, only for them, the Gnomes, to verbally identify her as 'Sin'. Once more, she then sought refuge in Satan's brain, although she was permitted to remain only for a time. Palamabron and Elynittria returning, Elynittria approached Satan with 'all her singing women', whose wine Satan imbibed. Intoxicated and apparently angry with the 'author' of his actions now that he understands something of his hypocritic past, Satan drove Luetha from his brain, effecting a lasting separation. Luetha finishes her speech by emphasizing her own responsibility for the series of events and making a plea on behalf of Satan, who is pictured throughout in his Garden of Eden form (the serpent). By the end of her speech, it is clear that she hopes for a particular kind of illocutionary effect: from her position of relative powerlessness, she wants to take on the blame for Satan's crime, and her aim is to present what is appreciable as a persuasive case:

> ... I am the Author of this Sin! by my suggestion
> My Parent power Satan has committed this transgression.
> I loved Palamabron & I sought to approach his Tent,
> But beautiful Elynittria with her silver arrows repelld me.
> For her light is terrible to me. I fade before her immortal beauty.
> O wherefore doth a Dragon-form forth issue from my limbs
> To seize her new born son? Ah me! the wretched Leutha!
> This to prevent, entering the doors of Satans brain night after night
> Like sweet perfumes I stupified the masculine perceptions
> And kept only the feminine awake, hence rose his soft

38 The Bard's Song II

Delusory love to Palamabron: admiration join'd with envy
Cupidity unconquerable! my fault, when at noon of day
The Horses of Palamabron call'd for rest and pleasant death:
I sprang out of the breast of Satan, over the Harrow beaming
In all my beauty! that I might unloose the flaming steeds
As Elynittria use'd to do; but too well those living creatures
Knew that I was not Elynittria, and they brake the traces
But me, the servants of the Harrow saw not: but as a bow
Of varying colours on the hills; terribly rag'd the horses.
Satan astonishd, and with power above his own controll
Compell'd the Gnomes to curb the horses, & to throw banks of sand
Around the fiery flaming Harrow in labyrinthine forms.
And brooks between to intersect the meadows in their course.
The Harrow cast thick flames: Jehovah thunderd above:
Chaos & ancient night fled from beneath the fiery Harrow:
The Harrow cast thick flames & orb'd us round in concave fires
A Hell of our own making. see, its flames still gird me round.
Jehovah thunder'd above! Satan in pride of heart
Drove the fierce Harrow among the constellations of Jehovah
Drawing a third part in the fires as stubble north & south
To devour Albion and Jerusalem the Emanation of Albion
Driving the Harrow in Pitys paths. 'twas then, with our dark fires
Which now gird round us (O eternal torment) I form'd the Serpent
Of precious stones & gold turn'd poisons on the sultry wastes
The Gnomes in all that day spar'd not; they curs'd Satan bitterly.
To do unkind things in kindness! with power armd, to say
The most irritating things in the midst of tears and love
These are the stings of the Serpent! thus did we by them; till thus
They in return retaliated, and the Living Creatures maddend.
The Gnomes labourd. I weeping hid in Satans inmost brain;
But when the Gnomes refus'd to labour more, with blandishments
I came forth from the head of Satan! back the Gnomes recoil'd.
And call'd me Sin, and for a sign portentous held me. Soon
Day sunk and Palamabron return'd, trembling I hid myself
In Satans inmost Palace of his nervous fine wrought Brain:
For Elynittria met Satan with all her singing women.
Terrific in their joy & pouring wine of wildest power
They gave Satan their wine: indignant at the burning wrath.
Wild with prophetic fury his former life became like a dream
Cloth'd in the Serpents folds, in selfish holiness demanding purity
Being Most impure, self-condemn'd to eternal tears, he drove

Me from his inmost Brain & the doors clos'd with thunders sound
O Divine Vision who didst create the Female: to repose
The Sleepers of Beulah: pity the repentant Leutha. My
Sick Couch bears the dark shades of Eternal Death infolding
The Spectre of Satan. he furious refuses to repose in sleep
I humbly bow in all my Sin before the Throne Divine.
Not so the Sick-one; Alas what shall be done him to restore?
Who calls the Individual Law, Holy: and despises the Saviour
Glorying to involve Albions Body in fires of eternal War—

Now Leutha ceas'd: tears flow'd: but the Divine Pity supported her.

All is my fault! We are the Spectre of Luvah the murderer.
Of Albion: O Vala! O Luvah! O Albion! O lovely Jerusalem
The Sin was begun in Eternity, and will not rest to Eternity
Till two Eternitys meet together, Ah! lost! lost! lost! for ever!
(11.35-13.11, E105-107)

Having completed her speech, Luetha learns of Enitharmon's creating a space for Satan and seeks refuge in the tent of Enitharmon, who is clearly associated with the wretched of this mythology. The events that follow immediately on from this appear to amount to the reaction, part perlocutionary effect, to both Luetha's speech and Enitharmon's creating of a space for Satan, which we considered in the previous chapter. Before Luetha first speaks, Los offers a commentary on what he views as the beginning of the unhappiness. Emphasizing female jealousy, he blames Elynittria, while evoking the distinction between Hebraism and Hellenism. He begins by responding to the creation of Canaan, but quickly begins to foreshadow what we will learn about from Luetha:

Satan! Ah me! is gone to his own place, said Los! their God
I will not worship in their Churches, nor King in their Theatres
Elynittria! whence is this jealousy running along the mountains
British Women were not Jealous when Greek & Roman were jealous
Every thing in Eternity shines by its own Internal light: but thou
Darkenest every Internal light with the arrows of thy quiver
Bound up in the borns of jealousy to a deadly fading Moon
And Ocalythron binds the Sun into a Jealous Globe
That every thing is fixd Opake without Internal light (10.12–20, E104)

Now we learn that, as if to make amends for her actions, Elynttria, having heard Luetha's words, meets Luetha in her hiding place and takes her to Palamabron's bed. This seeming reconciliation, however, reaps only further aspects of the fallen world. Luetha bears 'the shadowy Spectre of Sleep & nam'd him Death' (13.40, E107). Luetha herself is the female will, but, now, at the end of the poem, she (in dreams) bears other Blakean female-will figures, amongst whom the most important are Rahab and one of her daughters, Tirzah.

Time

This is where the Bard's Song ceases, and it segues forwards rather deftly: as we shall see, Milton stresses the female will, having heard the song. We'll turn to Milton's response presently (and the idea of the female will), but we have leapt over a section of the Song: immediately prior to the account of the entry of Death into life, the Bard provides an account of how, having heard Luetha, the Assembly adds time to space, setting in motion six thousand years of human history. The juxtaposition of Luetha's speech and the creation of history emphasizes the connectedness between the two – what we think of as sacred history is the result of Luetha's speech.

Blake uses two vocabularies in his sacred historiography: he speaks 'Eyes of God', of which there are seven or sometimes eight, but also of different historical periods as 'Churches'. (The 'Eyes of God' also figure in the poem as 'the Seven Angels of the Presence', as we shall see.) The 'Churches', of which there are twenty-seven or potentially twenty-eight provide us with an account of history which parallels the period covered by fourth, fifth, sixth and seventh 'Eyes'.

The twenty-seven churches are identifiable with an equal number of heavens, which will also be associated with Beulah in the poem: we learn they are 'the Monstrous Churches of Beulah' (37.16, E137). In another description we are told that Los's sons labour against death 'through all/ The Twenty-seven Heavens *of* Beulah *in* Ulro' (27.44–45, E125, my emphases). Towards the end of the poem, we are provided with the names of the Heavens/Churches, partly derived from Genesis. The groups also have specific sexual identities; two of the three groups are also identifiable with specific characters, namely Rahab and Tirzah; and all twenty-seven are identifiable with another figure, the Covering Cherub. Importantly, there is also a clear association between Milton's person and the churches. These associations are revealed over the course of the remainder of the poem, and we shall come to each of them in turn.

Blake's earlier writings are largely focused on the figure of Orc: each 'Eye' is represented by a turn of the cycle associated with Orc, who embodies revolutionary vigour. Blake thinks of the sequence of churches as a history of tyranny, although, in his view, sacred history is a twin-track account of both ever-greater insight and ever-intensifying tyranny. Natural religion, which we shall consider in a moment, is crucial to that tyranny. 'Each major cycle begins with a revolt against tyranny, and gradually ages into a new tyranny as the pressure of natural religion gets stronger' (2005: 252), observes Frye. At the same time, sacred history is characterized by a linearity, which is the work of Los. The completion of the Seventh Eye, associated with Christ, is bound up with apocalypse. As Frye explains, 'The apocalypse proper begins with the French and American revolutions, when the revolutionary iconoclasm of Orc, which was made manifest in Jesus, returns to complete the seventh cycle' (2004: 137). But Blake also extends his thinking to the Eighth eye: 'The Second Coming of Jesus, which ends history, introduces an eighth (Albion or redeemed man)', explains Frye. As we shall see, Milton is also associated with this Eighth Eye.

Act of Mercy

The Mundane Egg sits at the centre of the world of the fallen zoas in the design of plate 32. It is not emphasized in *Milton*, but the creation of the Mundane Shell and Egg between Molech and Elohim (the second and third Eye) must also stem from the foregoing events which conclude with Luetha's speech. 'The Mundane Egg', observes Damon, 'is this three-dimensional world of time and space, in which fallen Man incubates until he hatches and re-enters Eternity' (1988: 288). The inner side of the Mundane Egg is represented by the 'mundane Shell' (4.3, E97) which Los builds around what Blake calls the 'Polypus', emblem of natural life, humanity without 'Human Form' (24.37, E120). The heavens of the Mundane Shell are the twenty-seven heavens/ Churches we just spoke of. As well as its twenty-seven dimensions, the inside of Mundane Egg has three personifications associated with it:

> The Mundane Shell, is a vast Concave Earth: an immense
> Hardend shadow of all things upon our Vegetated Earth
> Enlarg'd into dimension & deform'd into indefinite space;
> In Twenty-seven Heavens and all their Hells; with Chaos
> And Ancient Night; & Purgatory. It is a cavernous Earth
> Of labyrinthine intricacy, twenty-seven folds of opakeness
> (17.21–26, E110–111)

As Damon explains, the Shell is to man's physical existence what the churches are to his spiritual life, 'an enclosure which shuts him from

Eternity' (1998: 85), but, as he also points out, 'Los creates the Egg as a protection' (1988: 288).

The Bard's history stresses the importance of another factor which is characterized by a sense of a guiding intelligence. Blake is careful to provide details about *limits* to the Fall. Also a response to Luetha's words, the worlds of Satan and Adam come into existence between Molech and Elohim: the 'Divine Hand' forms 'the Two Limits: first of Opacity [Satan], then of Contraction [Adam]' (13.20, E107), which establishes limits. (Speaking of the design of plate 32, Paley observes that 'Adam, appropriately, is entirely in the circle of Urthona, for man is capable of being regenerated through the indwelling Christ of the Imagination; while Satan straddles the other three Zoas, the ruined world created by the fall' (1970: 240–241).) Summing up these interrelated developments, Frye makes the following sequence of important observations:

> Adam in Blake is the physical man, the soul in the form of the bodies we now see. He is called the "Limit of Contraction": that is, he has fallen as far as man can without losing his imagination altogether and the ability to recreate himself along with it. Along with this creation went the completion of the present universe, which Blake calls the "Mundane Shell". (2004: 132–133)

In the Bard's Song the emphasis has been on speech which exacerbates alienation, driving humanity further from its original condition, or on failed performatives, which produce the same effect. But by setting history in motion in this way, the 'Assembly', in response to Luetha's words, has already started the process of possible regeneration. There is clearly something providential in how the Elect are to be treated; because they are not subjected to Eternal Death, there *will* be an end to history. Similarly, life falls no further than Adam and Satan, which also speaks to a possible restoration. Sacred history is 'comedic', in the sense that it will, after a time, conclude with restoration. But it is not until Milton hears the Bard's Song that the last act begins.

Milton's Reaction to the Song

The narrative (the *syuzhet*) picks up where it left off before the Bard's Song – the Bard's Song provides an account of all the earlier developments, and now *syuzhet* simply proceeds with the events representing the continuation of the *fabula*. In other words, we return to the instant which is the poem's focus, though, in a sense we have never left it: the events cover thousands of years, but their narration is part of the instant.

The Bard's Song itself is a speech act which is separable from the rest of Blake's epic, and we might begin with an important general observation about it. The song might be mistaken for a constative speech act – that is how I presented it a moment ago, in fact, when summing up everything that gets accounted for in the song. Up to a point, it *is* constative, but, as we shall see now in the final section of this chapter, it also possesses performative power.

Interestingly, on completing his Song, it is demanded of the Bard that he explain how he knows what he has spoken of, and the Bard must (briefly) speak once more. A power structure is clearly perceptible. We are told that the Bard begins his song when 'sitting at eternal tables,/ Terrific among the sons of Albion in chorus solemn & loud' (2:23–24, E96). The question has the power of a sociopolitical performative speech act, specifically a command: 'Where hadst thou this terrible Song' (13:50, E107). The command invokes a sense of hierarchy, inscribing the Bard as one who obeys, but he fearlessly claims full divine inspiration for the song in a performative which, with his prophetic tone, effects his independence from the apparent sociopolitical structures and positions him as a creator in his own right, inspired by a higher power:

... I am Inspired! I know it is the Truth! For I Sing
According to the inspiration of the Poetic genius
Who is the eternal all-protecting Divine Humanity
To whom be Glory & Power & Dominion Evermore Amen
(13:51–14:3, E107–108)

Hence, the song also impresses the reader as a phenomenological performative. Indeed, it is not simply *like* the creative Word; the Bard is claiming that his song is inspired by that Word. He does not have the *creative* power of the divine Word, but he has its authority.

Milton's reaction to it represents the song's most important perlocutionary effect. As a result of his hearing the song, Milton's viewpoint is revolutionized, and he resolves to take decisive action. Of course the Bard's Song also has the effect of making him speak – we only know of the revolution and resolution because Milton is inspired to deliver an important soliloquy, ultimately inseparable from his decision.

The Song produces a cataclysmic response in Eternity, and the Bard seeks refuge in Milton's bosom. Milton then removes the 'robe of the promise' and detaches himself from 'the oath of God' (14.13, E108), whereupon he begins to soliloquize:

> ... I go to Eternal Death. The Nations still
> Follow after the detestable Gods of Priam; in pomp
> Of warlike selfhood, contradicting and blaspheming.
> When will the Resurrection come; to deliver the sleeping body
> From corruptibility: O when Lord Jesus wilt thou come?
> Tarry no longer; for my soul lies at the gates of death.
> I will arise and look forth for the morning of the grave.
> I will go down to the sepulcher to see if morning breaks!
> I will go down to self annihilation and eternal death,
> Lest the Last Judgment come & find me unannihilate
> And I be siez'd & giv'n into the hands of my own Selfhood
> The Lamb of God is seen thro' mists & shadows, hov'ring
> Over the sepulchers in clouds of Jehovah & winds of Elohim
> A disk of blood, distant; & heav'ns & earth's roll dark between
> What do I here before the Judgment? without my Emanation?
> With the daughters of memory, & not with the daughters of inspiration[?]
> I in my Selfhood am that Satan: I am that Evil One!
> He is my Spectre! in my obedience to loose him from my Hells
> To claim the Hells, my furnaces, I go to Eternal Death. (14.14–32, E108)

Much of Milton's own vision has been corrected by the content of the Song: his ideas about Sin and Death, as well as his understanding of the three classes. But it is the figure of Satan that makes the most significant impact on him. Most importantly, he senses the identity between his own Spectre and Satan.

We can only understand the perlocutionary effect of the Bard's Song as a whole by means of a close reading of this speech. In the first instance, most of the required commentary is commentary on the last five lines of Milton's speech, where the theme is Spectre and emanation. Having provided a comprehensive commentary on those lines, however, we will return to the opening lines, which also require special consideration.

Spectre and Emanation

As Frye states, Blake is a decidedly schematic thinker. Crucial to the above speech is the contrast between what Blake calls the spectre and emanation, which form a pair. In Chapter 3, we will see that these two belong to a fourfold schema as well, but in the first instance we may treat the two as a separate opposition.

In connection with idealized experience, Blake stresses the importance of looking inside oneself, where one finds the power to love and therefore to transform or create. Here the main faculty is the imagination, or what Frye calls 'forming power' (2005: 295). In *There is No Natural Religion*, Blake states 'Mans perceptions are not bounded by organs of perception. he perceives more than sense (tho' ever so acute) can discover' (E2). The imagination impacts on two aspects of the world around us: first, on the natural environment, and, second, on the people we love. In relation to nature, we must look inside ourselves for the imaginative vision of the paradise to be regained, and then go to work in the external world trying to bring it into existence, thereby restoring nature. 'Creation releases desire' (Frye, 2005: 234), as Frye says. And in relation to the emotional life, looking inside oneself is equally important. Nothing is really lovable is Blake's suggestion. *Lovingfulness* transforms the object into something lovable and therefore beloved.

In our world, the drama of mankind and nature, on the one hand, and the relations between lovers, on the other, are separate and distinct, but in Blake's poetry they are two aspects of the same metaphorical cluster. In Blake's condensed vision, the idealized female figure, the Emanation in his vocabulary, is unfallen nature, but also the symbolically female counterpart of the lover. As Frye puts it, the Emanation is 'the total form of all the things a man loves and creates' (2004: 78).

A distinction between different idealized emanations is required, however. If we revisit Blake's conceptions of Eden and Beulah, in connection with this point, in Blake's thinking, Eden, the upper-most world of a manifold universe, is the world of fulfilled desire, and it is characterized by a unity of creator and creature, and form and energy, which is also a unity of male and female principles. But, as we know, a lower heaven is also crucial to Blake's thought: beneath the higher heaven is the lower paradise named Beulah. As Frye expertly explains, in the former, male and female are creator and creature, in the latter, lover and bride:

> In the highest or Paradisal view of reality (Eden), man is one with God, and everything else is part of a divine, and therefore a human, creation. Imagination attempts to recreate the world in the form in which man originally possessed it. In the next highest view, which is sexual rather than fully human (*M*, pl. 4, l. 5), the view of the lower Paradise or Beulah, the relation of creator and creature becomes the relation of lover and beloved, and the created world becomes an "emanation" or responsive bride, like Shelley's epipsyche. (Frye, 2005: 243)

(Especially significant is the fact that on the highest level the agent which is the spectre on lower levels is not 'natural' or even 'sexual' but 'human'.)

The descent from the upper levels of reality is associated with a separation of those male and female principles, 'contraries' in Blake's language. Central to Blake's understanding of fallenness is the figure of the Spectre, the reason-using fallen human. As Frye explains, the Spectre makes the mistake of looking *outside* of itself for gratification. The faculty it uses when looking outside itself is not the imagination but reason. In *There is No Natural Religion*, Blake speaks of reason as both sense experience and abstract thought. Reason is 'the ratio', an unstable faculty which forever changes as new experience inevitably necessitates new intellectual conclusions. Reason 'tries to control or suppress desire in the name of order' (Frye, 2005: 234). Through the power of reason, the Spectre seeks to understand the laws of nature, and, having found them, it advocates laws for human life modelled on the laws of nature, so that human life may eventually achieve the condition in which it is as *ordered* as nature. As Frye explains,

> Intellectually, the Spectre works with abstractions, trying to understand nature by patterns and diagrams. These have no power to order life, but the Spectre cannot realize that, and keeps trying to fit human life to nature by imitating nature's regularity, or law. The result of this is morality, the futile attempt to make the reasonable desirable. (ibid.)

And in relation to the emotional life, looking outside oneself is equally self-defeating. 'Emotionally and sexually, the Spectre is a "ravening devouring lust", looking outside himself for gratification, instead of understanding that everything he can love is his "Emanation", loved by virtue of his capacity to love' (2005: 234), explains Frye.

We have already come across how Blake associated Newton and Locke with one another, and the association is of great relevance in this context. In Blake's world, Newton is the champion of a mechanical universe, while Blake associates Locke with the psychology of the Spectre, which as well as being self-defeating is also mechanical. Blake makes connections between the two Englishmen 'because the mechanistic universe of the one and the mechanistic psychology of the other fitted perfectly' (Damon, 1988: 298).

Again, the two aspects belong to a single metaphorical cluster. The counterpart may (confusingly) be referred to as an emanation, but she is the 'female will', a Blakean figure which may refer to nature, with its apparent agency, or the person the spectral self is (unhappily) emotionally tied to.

With respect to the opening of *Milton*, it is the second metaphorical cluster which is important. Milton experiences a revelation about his own identity. His self is a spectral self – it is actually identifiable with Satan. His female counterpart is the female will, his loved ones and his world, 'the total body of what he can love and create, outside himself instead of inside' (Frye, 2005: 359). His counterpart comprises 'daughters of memory' rather than 'daughters of inspiration' (14.29, E108). Blake has already introduced us to this distinction in the preface to the poem. The former are suggestive of Hellenism, clearly anathema to Blake; the latter speak to Blake's Hebraism. In his soliloquy, however, what Milton emphasizes is the *absence* of his Emanation – an Edenic Emanation. In other moments in the poem, it is clear that the problem is his being *in possession* of a fallen-world emanation. In Book II, Milton, who by this time has a sense of the contrast between his real self and his Spectre, speaks of how his Spectre continues to wander in search of his Emanation:

> I have turned my back upon these Heavens builded on cruelty
> My Spectre still wandering thro' them follows my Emanation
> He hunts her footsteps thro' the snow & the wintry hail & rain
> (32.3–5, E131)

(Such a female figure is clearly a figure of 'mystery', an association we shall return to.) And before he first speaks, he views his 'Sixfold Emanation scattr'd thro' the deep' (2.19, E96). The 'Sixfold Emanation' suggests the three women whom he married in different periods of his life (Elizabeth Minshull, Katherine Woodcock and Mary Powell) and three of his daughters (Anne, Mary and Deborah). (It is just possible to make out the presence of the six in the design of the plate 1(3). They adorn the title letters.) In his sonnet XXIII, 'On His Deceasd Wife', Katherine Woodcock appears in Milton's fancy, emanating 'love, sweetness, [and] goodness', but Blake chooses to emphasize the general point that Milton had fraught relations with the women in his life.

The imagery tells us about his relationship with the women in his life but also, owing to the metaphorical nature of the imagery, about his attitude to the natural environment. In Blake's condensed vision, the Sixfold emanation is also *identifiable* with the external world as Milton sees it and relates to it.

Nature, Religion and War

For Blake, the opposite of natural is 'revealed', and in his view, the only real religion is revealed religion. But even if the only real religion is revealed, Blake is aware of the fact that his contemporaries accept the external world as the basis of one's religion. The worship of nature is 'natural religion' in Blake's lexicon.

Blake's conclusion is that Milton's Christianity is the reason his world is still in the power of the 'female will'. Milton was a Puritan, and we typically think of Puritanism as a movement seeking to establish the purest possible Protestant Church in England, purging the Church of England of the last vestiges of Roman Catholicism in the process. Unsurprisingly, Blake promotes an unconventional understanding of Puritanism. As Frye explains, for Blake, Puritanism involves a strong admixture of natural religion, which in the eighteenth century takes the form of Deism.

> Puritanism was the ancestor of Deism in the sense that everything wrong with Puritanism, its vestigial natural religion, its Pharisaic morality, its scholastic rationalism, and its belief in the infallible goodness of the conventionally orthodox, had in the following century been precipitated as Deism. (2004: 329)

Puritanism insists on the separateness of the divine and the human, which is incompatible with the imagination. In Blake's view, 'Man in his creative acts and perceptions is God, and God is Man' (Frye, 2004: 37). But where the contrast between the divine and the human is insisted upon, God gets demoted to an 'abstract spectre' and under such conditions, rather than seeing as He sees, humanity can only withdraw to sense experience (Frye, 2004: 240).

One of the most striking themes introduced in Milton's speech is the connection between Puritanism and war: he speaks of them in the same breath, and the former seems to bear a causal relationship to the latter. He begins the speech by surveying contemporary history. Paley expertly sums up the first two levels of history in the poem:

> In the seventeenth century, John Milton as Secretary of State was deeply engaged in international political activities for the Commonwealth, serving before, during, and after Oliver Cromwell's ascendancy. "Charles calls on Milton for Atonement. Cromwell is ready" (5.39, E99). The "artillery" (Blake's only use of the word) beneath which Satan "fainted" (5.2, E98) recalls both

Satan's invention of cannon in *Paradise Lost* – the word "artillery" is not used there – and the New Model Army's famously successful use of artillery to reduce royalist strongholds formerly thought impregnable. The wars of Milton's time are repeated for Blake in the Anglo-French war that resumed on 18 March 1803, after the abrogation of the Treaty of Amiens by both sides. (2011: 802)

Blake is of the view that Milton's failure is of the utmost seriousness. Crucially, Milton's natural religion was the harbinger of both the religion and the war of Blake's times. The fact that Deism leaves us in the hands of our spectres is essential. The spectre is the death-wish in human life, and war or sacrifice is what it produces:

> In Deism there is not only the belief that the physical world is the real one, but also a feeling of satisfaction at remaining within it, a certain enthusiasm about accepting the conditions it imposes. Now it seems reasonable enough to take the world as we find it, trying to be as contented in it as possible, and make others so, without straining after more elusive pleasures, perhaps less substantial ones. But if it were possible to do this the human race would have settled into Utopian serenity centuries ago. It remains true that the physical world is not good enough for the imagination to accept, and if we do accept it we are left with our Selfhoods, our venomous crawling egos that spend all their time either wronging others or brooding on wrongs done to them. The end of all natural religion, however, well-meaning and good-natured, is a corrupt and decadent society rolling downhill to stampeding mass hysteria and maniacal warfare. (Frye, 2004: 73)

Wittreich may be right when he suggests that, in contrast to 'Milton the poet', 'Milton the pamphleteer' (1975: 240) is committed to 'mental fight', but Milton now realizes that his own epics supported war. As James observes, Milton 'admits that his own epic failed to turn the energies of men from material to mental warfare' and concedes 'the necessary connection between the subject matter of the classical epic and the kind of society it reflected and produced' (1978: 74).

Departure From Heaven

We can safely conclude that, having heard the Bard's Song, Milton becomes aware of each of the foregoing points: their realization is a mental revolution, and that revolution is, as we have said, part of the perlocutionary effect of the song. The effects do not stop there, however. As we see from the speech, as a consequence of his newly acquired knowledge, Milton resolves to quit heaven: 'I go to Eternal Death'. Taylor argues convincingly that, while it represents a part of the complex perlocutionary effect of the Bard's Song, Milton's words amount to another performative statement, even though the verb chosen is merely a verb of motion. (Typically, a future time adverbial would be used when pressing a verb of motion into this kind of function, Taylor explains; not using such an adverbial 'increases the forcefulness, the daring of the act', he argues (1979: 46).) As Fallon has argued, '*Milton* as a whole inverts the conventional apotheosis, with Milton rejecting heaven and returning to earth' (2017: 238).

If Milton can succeed, he will transform his religion into something far greater than his Puritanism – or Deism, for that matter. A personal dimension will inhere in the vision: success in his quest will involve his achieving a *human* identity which may entail a different way of visualizing women. As Frye says, 'one is struck by the fact that Milton never sees beyond the sinister "female will"' (2004: 343). But his quest is not purely personal. Within the confines of Blake's imagination, where everything is taking place, the further development of Milton's personality will clearly be of social consequence. As Erdman explains, Blake originally planned a longer, historical epic dealing with how the failure of the Puritan revolution led to the troubles of Blake's times (1969: 423). References to James and Charles survived, but Blake reduces history to what he takes to be the prime mover: Milton's faith. For Blake, Milton was the spearhead of that revolution, its visionary; his failures spelled failure for society, so his biography is all the history that is required. But if Milton can achieve a new vision and a new faith, mankind may be able to rise out of its fallen condition.

References

Blake, W. (1988), *The Complete Poetry and Prose of William Blake: Newly Revised Edition*, ed. D. V. Erdman, University of California Press: Berkeley.
Bloom, H. (1982), 'Commentary' in *The Complete Poetry and Prose of William Blake*, ed. D.V. Erdman, Berkeley: University of California Press, 894–972.
Damon, S.F. (1988), *A Blake Dictionary: The Ideas and Symbols of William Blake*, Hanover: University Press of New England.
Erdman, D. (1969), *Prophet Against Empire: A Poet's Interpretation of the History of His Own Times*, Princeton: Princeton University Press.

Fallon, D. (2017), *Blake, Myth, and Enlightenment: The Politics of Apotheosis.* Houndmills: Palgrave.

Fox, S. (1976), *Poetic Form in Blake's Milton*, Princeton: Princeton University Press.

Frye, N. (2004), *Fearful Symmetry: A Study of William Blake*, ed. N. Halmi, Toronto: University of Toronto Press.

Frye, N. (2005), *Northrop Frye on Milton and Blake*, ed. A. Esterhammer, Toronto: University of Toronto Press.

James, D. (1977), *Written Within and Without: A Study of Blake's Milton*, Frankfurt: Peter Lang.

Paley, M. (1970), *Energy and Imagination: A Study of the Development of Blake's Thought*, Oxford: Clarendon Press.

Paley, M. (2011), 'William Blake's *Milton/A Poem* and the Miltonic Matrix of 1791–1810'. *University of Toronto Quarterly* 80.4. (2011): 786–814.

Taylor, R.C. (1979), 'Semantic Structures and the Temporal Modes of Blake's Prophetic Verse', *Language and Style* 12: 26–49.

Wittreich, J. (1975), *Angel of Apocalypse: Blake's Idea of Milton*, Wisconsin: University of Wisconsin.

3 'the forward path/ Of Milton's journey' and the Opponents of His Progress

Our next focus is the speeches made by the Blakean figures who encounter Milton's journeying redeemed self. The performative speech now falls into the pattern which ultimately guarantees the completeness of the instant: the speech of the agents on the side of mankind proves effective, while the speech of opponents fails to achieve its end.

Before we turn to the speech acts in this section, a little context is required: specifically, we need to consider Milton's initial journey before his redeemed self begins to encounter the zoas.

The Journeying Milton: Context II

Milton's personality gets disaggregated in the poem, and it is a manifold Milton we meet in the next part of Book I, even though his redeemed self will emerge as the main focus of the action. In Chapter 2, we came across the Spectre and the Emanation. In another arrangement, these two figures belong to a schema employed by Blake which includes a total of four aspects: Shadow, Spectre, Emanation and Humanity. In Chapter 1 of Blake's *Jerusalem*, he speaks of these four as different dimensions of Albion:

> I see the Four-fold Man. The Humanity in its deadly sleep
> And its fallen Emanation. The spectre & its cruel Shadow.
> (Chapter 1, 15:6–7, E159)

In *Milton*, Blake uses all four terms in connection with his protagonist. In Chapters 1 and 2, we considered Blake's understanding of the spiritual class system, where the important groups are Elect, Redeemed and Reprobate. Blake discusses Milton using these vocabularies as well. Also important are Milton's 'spirit' and his body, spoken of as opposition between his mortal and immortal parts. As we shall see, Blake combines

DOI: 10.4324/9781003342571-4

these different vocabularies when speaking of the many aspects of Milton, sometimes using two terms for a single aspect of self.

As we have seen, Milton resolves to go to 'Eternal Death', having understood that Satan is his spectre. The vehicle of his journey is his Shadow. It will also be said that he is entering his 'Own Vortex' (15.22, E109), and his vehicle will be spoken of as a 'Cloud' (37.16, E137) in the finale of the poem – the full-page design on the title page could depict either or both. We learn that the Twenty-Seven Heavens identifiable with the Churches are also identifiable with Milton's Shadow, which stretches all the way to Britain:

> Then on the verge of Beulah he beheld his own Shadow;
> A mournful form double; hermaphroditic: male & female
> In one wonderful body. and he enterd into it
> In direful pain for the dread shadow, twenty-seven-fold
> Reachd to the depths of direst Hell, & thence to Albions land.
> (14.36–40, E108)

It is significant that his Shadow is described as 'hermaphroditic', although we should consider this point at the right time.

If we treat his emanation as a separate phenomenon for now, we can say that, in addition to the Shadow, three aspects of Milton's personality – Humanity, redeemed self and body – are central to the next section of the poem. The focus immediately shifts to Milton's Humanity, which gets identified as his 'real and immortal Self'. Milton enters into his Shadow, but he retains an Edenic self, or Humanity. Those in Eternity see him as 'One sleeping on a couch of gold', and he himself is afforded the vision of his continued existence in Eden, where he moves like a sleepwalker:

> As when a man dreams, he reflects not that his body sleeps,
> Else he would wake; so seem'd he entering his Shadow: but
> With him the Spirits of the Seven Angels of the Presence
> Entering; they gave him still perceptions of his Sleeping Body;
> Which now arose and walk'd with them in Eden, as an Eighth
> Image Divine tho' darken'd; and tho walking as one walks
> In sleep; and the Seven comforted and supported him.
>
> Like as a Polypus that vegetates beneath the deep!
> They saw his Shadow vegetated underneath the Couch
> Of death: for when he enterd into his Shadow: Himself
> His real and immortal Self: was as appeard to those

54 *'the forward path/ Of Milton's journey'*

> Who dwell in immortality, as One sleeping on a couch
> Of gold; and those in immortality gave forth their Emanations
> Like Females of sweet beauty, to guard round him & to feed
> His lips with food of Eden in his cold and dim repose!. (15:1-15, E109)

Blake leaves this aspect of Milton's identity in Eden to switch back to Milton beginning his descent by entering his Shadow. We have been told that Milton's Shadow passes through hell and proceeds to 'Albions land', and Milton's journey follows that path:

> Onwards his Shadow kept its course among the Spectres; call'd
> Satan, but swift as lightning passing them, startled the shades
> Of Hell beheld him in a trail of light as of a comet
> That travels into Chaos ... (15.17-20, E109)

(The design of plate 32 visualizes Milton's descent – of course in the design he *rises upwards*, through Satan to Adam.) Then, in a passage that has elicited an enormous amount of commentary but which needs no extended commentary in this reading, it is clarified that 'the heaven' his redeemed self has emerged from and the earth it is approaching are vortices, the former a vortex he has passed through, the latter 'A vortex not yet pass'd' (15.35, E109). Earth heaving into view, his descent is tied in with both his seeing Albion and Blake's first encounter with Milton – which we shall return to in the next chapter. Because in Blake's mythology, the Atlantic kingdom was deluged, Blake thinks of the fallen world as the 'Sea of Space and Time'. The only dry land in this place is the 'Rock of Ages' (Britain), and the fallen Albion is pictured as 'A Giant form of perfect beauty outstretchd on the rock'. Having taken in the sight of the fallen Albion, Milton falls into our world:

> First Milton saw Albion upon the Rock of Ages,
> Deadly pale outstretchd and snowy cold, storm coverd;
> A Giant form of perfect beauty outstretchd on the rock
> In solemn death: the Sea of Time & Space thunderd aloud
> Against the rock, which was inwrapped with the weeds of death
> Hovering over the cold bosom, in its vortex Milton bent down
> To the bosom of death, what was underneath soon seemd above.
> A cloudy heaven mingled with stormy seas in loudest ruin;
> But as a wintry globe descends precipitant thro' Beulah bursting,

With thunders loud and terrible: so Miltons shadow fell
Precipitant loud thundring into the Sea of Time & Space.
(15.36–46, E109–110)

This segues to a scene in which Milton unites with Blake, which we'll also turn to in Chapter 4, and then a scene in which Milton's redeemed self develops a new understanding of his wives and daughters, and how they see from 'eternal spheres'. As we have seen, Milton refers to his emanation after having listened to the Bard's song. His relationship with his family is spoken of in dysphoric terms: his being in heaven without his emanation gets causally connected to his fraught temporal relations with his wives and daughters. (See the upper section of the design of plate 16 for Blake depiction of Milton's wives and daughters.) The focus now shifting to them, we are provided with a different perspective. The only way to enter Beulah is through its gates or 'Heavens'. Already in the poem, these heavens have been spoken of in relation to the Daughters of Albion:

And this is the manner of the Daughters of Albion in their beauty
Every one is threefold in Head & Heart & Reins, & every one
Has three Gates into the Three Heavens of Beulah which shine
Translucent in their Foreheads & their Bosoms & their Loins.
(5.5–9, E98)

When his redeemed self sees his wives and daughters now, he is capable of understanding that it was only through his wives and daughters that he knew anything of the Three Heavens of Beulah in his lifetime. This insight shifts perspective because now the emphasis is moved to the fact that their fraught relations exist on a lower plane, and that, his family, like Milton himself, is desperately in need of redemption, which might also be eventuated by Milton's 'giving up of Selfhood'. (Bracher argues that there is a clear casual link between Milton's uniting with Blake and his improved perception of his own biography (1985: 85–86).) The focus rests on the 'conflict with those Female Forms', which is captured through three different rhetorical strategies. First, through the wives and daughters being identified with the female-will figures born in dreams at the end of the Bard's Song – Rahab and her daughters, whose names are those of the daughters of Zelophehad (Numbers 27: 1-1); second, through simile ('They sat rangd round him as the rocks of Horeb round the land', etc.); and finally via a further metaphorical flourish ('and his body was the Rock Sinai', etc.). And of course the Milton who emerges here is, as Bloom observes, a 'Mosaic

Milton'. But the most important idea to emerge is that his wives and daughters, like Milton, are 'Human', despite their condition. It is in this context that we also come across the first reference to Milton's 'body', the third aspect of self relevant here:

> Then Milton knew that the Three Heavens of Beulah were beheld
> By him on earth in his bright pilgrimage of sixty years
> In those three females whom his Wives, & those three whom his Daughters
> Had represented and containd, that they might be resum'd
> By giving up of Selfhood: & they distant view'd his journey
> In their eternal spheres, now Human, tho' their Bodies remain clos'd
> In the dark Ulro till the Judgment: also Milton knew: they and
> Himself was Human, tho' now wandering thro Death's Vale
> In conflict with those Female forms, which in blood & jealousy
> Surrounded him, dividing & uniting without end or number.
>
> He saw the Cruelties of Ulro, and he wrote them down
> In iron tablets: and his Wives & Daughters names were these
> Rahab and Tirzah, & Milcah & Malah & Noah & Hoglah,
> They sat rangd round him as the rocks of Horeb round the land
> Of Canaan: and they wrote in thunder smoke and fire
> His dictate; and his body was the Rock Sinai; that body,
> Which was on earth born to corruption: & the six Females
> Are Hor & Peor & Bashan & Abarim & Lebanon & Hermon
> Seven rocky masses terrible in the Desarts of Midian. (15.51–17.17, E110)

Humanity, redeemed self and body: these aspects are of primary significance at first. The redeemed self is the main focus of the remainder of the section of the poem under consideration and therefore the focus for the rest of this chapter. In Book II, this aspect will be identified as Milton's 'thought' only, but for now it is the most salient dimension.

In the poem, the focus quickly shifts to *responses* to Milton's journeying redeemed self. It will be clarified that Milton is not simply descending to Ulro; he is going to Golgonooza (19.24–26, E113) – his journey is characterized by the same double terminus that Ololon's is, as we shall see in Chapter 5. The zoas offer verbal resistance to his progress. Fortunately, their performatives will prove ineffective – at least in terms of stopping Milton or worsening his predicament when he has started to fight with Urizen.

These struggles can only be treated separately, but they are simultaneous, and though the speech acts seem sequential, they must be understood as simultaneous as well, whatever the offence to our sense of what constitutes an act. Fox sums up the unitary nature of the segments discussed in the main part of this chapter:

> Milton, embracing the shadow that is this mortal life, must resist its lures and transcend its delusions in order to redeem it. That is his struggle with the female will, his struggle with Urizen. Each facet of Milton's struggle contains the whole struggle; each is a battle of the fourfold with the twofold soul. (1976: 85)

The speeches of Enitharmon, the Shadowy Female, Orc, Rahab and Tirzah will be treated individually, but, in a deeper sense, they are all aspects of the same – largely verbal – act.

Enitharmon and Los; the Shadowy Female and Orc

Los (the fallen Urthona) and Enitharmon, his emanation, are first. The Milton they see appears like a comet in the sky, journeying and falling. Enitharmon has a sense that Milton wishes to liberate Satan from his hells, which, she thinks, will give Satan the chance to persecute the fallen Albion. When, in the next passage of arms, Rintrah and Palamabron react to Los's arrival with Milton, they also express fear about how Milton's mission will lead to Satan's persecuting Albion after Satan is freed; in that iteration, it is clear that this persecution will follow on from Orc's being liberated by Milton (22.31-35, E117). Enitharmon also believes that Milton is coming to free *her*. She is the first to resort to speech in response to Milton:

> Los the Vehicular terror beheld him, & divine Enitharmon
> Call'd all her daughters, Saying. Surely to unloose my bond
> Is this Man come! Satan shall be unloosd upon Albion (17.31-33, E111)

The perlocutionary effect of Enitharmon's words is represented by Los's response. Later in Book I, Los will understand the significance of Milton's descent; in the first instance, he is perturbed by Enitharmon's short speech about her bond being eliminated. Reacting to her words, he offers physical resistance to Milton:

58 'the forward path/ Of Milton's journey'

> Los heard in terror Enitharmons words: in fibrous strength
> His limbs shot forth like roots of trees against the forward path
> Of Miltons journey. (17.34–36, E111)

(Los is pictured as a half-human, half-tree figure in the design of plate 16, where this moment is visualized. Urizen also resists the progress of Milton, but, strikingly, only his head is pictured in this design. Is he emerging from the earth?)

The other three fallen zoas also see Milton (though little is made of Tharmas's seeing him), and first to respond is Orc along with the 'Shadowy Female', both of whom speak. Just as Orc is the fallen Luvah, the Shadowy Female is the fallen version of Luvah's emanation, Vala. Readers of Blake's earlier poems know a little about the story of Orc and the Shadowy Female, and much of that is clearly relevant in this poem. Even though it is not emphasized in any way in this rendering, it becomes clear in the remainder of *Milton* that, as in Blake's earlier poetry, owing to jealousy, Los has bound Orc down with a 'chain of Jealousy' (63.16, E343); in the earlier poetry, this is quite clearly on a mountain-top. Los, along with Enitharmon, have regretted their actions but have found they have no power to release Orc (62.21–63.6, E342–343).

Unlike the next characters to address Milton, neither the Shadowy Female nor Orc directly addresses Milton. They agonistically address each other. But it becomes clear that, owing to the Shadowy Female's unwillingness to yield to Orc's will, she represents a threat to Milton's progress.

What the Shadowy Female and the bound Orc say to each other in *Milton* is structured around the opposition of physical organization ('Form') and garments ('Clothing'). ('If there is a single central image in *Milton*', observes Bloom, 'it is the garment' (1963: 396).) We should not forget that on a very rudimentary level, Orc is fallen humanity and the Shadowy Female is fallen nature. The distinction between form and clothing allows Blake to explore the double nature of nature. Here, forms are not male or female but 'Human' or female. Moreover, the human is also divine. The exchange between the two revolves around how the Shadowy Female should take on the divine: whether she should adopt a Human and therefore divine Form, or whether her garment should be 'a Garment of Pity & Compassion like the Garment of God'. In the case of the former, the garment is 'Cruelty'. In the case of the latter, she must take on a 'Female Form'. The nature of the human condition is bound up with this combination of forms and attire. She is resolved to take on the human and divine form, and all the misery of fallen life is pictured in the garment she would wear. Famine, pestilence and war are its chief features. She is a hypocritical figure: 'The Shadowy Female', observes Bracher, '... makes ... cruelty seem a mere cover, a garment, while underneath she puts on a Human Form of pity and love ... providing the occasion for her supposed pity/ love to manifest itself to greatest advantage' (1985: 93). The garment proves identifiable with both Satan and the Covering Cherub. In a reference to their shared past, she suggests that her garments will also protect her from Orc's terrors:

> I will lament over Milton in the lamentations of the afflicted
> My Garments shall be woven of sighs & heart broken lamentations
> The misery of unhappy Families shall be drawn out into its border
> Wrought with the needle with dire sufferings poverty pain & woe
> Along the rocky Island & thence throughout the whole Earth
> There shall be the sick Father & his starving Family! there
> The Prisoner in the stone Dungeon & the Slave at the Mill
> I will have Writings written all over it in Human Words
> That every Infant that is born upon the Earth shall read
> And get by rote as a hard task of a life of sixty years
> I will have Kings inwoven upon it, & Councellors & Mighty Men
> The Famine shall clasp it together with buckles & Clasps
> And the Pestilence shall be its fringe & the War its girdle
> To divide into Rahab & Tirzah that Milton may come to our tents
> For I will put on the Human Form & take the Image of God
> Even Pity & Humanity but my Clothing shall be Cruelty
> And I will put on Holiness as a breastplate & as a helmet
> And all my ornaments shall be of the gold of broken hearts
> And the precious stones of anxiety & care & desperation & death
> And repentance for sin & sorrow & punishment & fear
> To defend me from thy terrors O Orc! my only beloved!
>
> Orc answerd. Take not the Human Form O loveliest. Take not
> Terror upon thee! Behold how I am & tremble lest thou also
> Consume in my Consummation; but thou maist take a Form
> Female & lovely, that cannot consume in Mans consummation
> Wherefore dost thou Create & Weave this Satan for a Covering
> When thou attemptest to put on the Human Form, my wrath
> Burns to the top of heaven against thee in Jealousy & Fear.
> Then I rend thee asunder, then I howl over thy clay & ashes
> When wilt thou put on the Female Form as in times of old
> With a Garment of Pity & Compassion like the Garment of God

His garments are long sufferings for the Children of Men
Jerusalem is his Garment & not thy Covering Cherub O lovely
Shadow of my delight who wanderest seeking for the prey.
(18:8–18:38, E111)

Fox suggests that 'Los and Orc seek to thwart their emanations, Los by putting out barriers to stop Milton from approaching, and Orc by trying to dissuade the Shadowy Female from luring him on' (1976: 79). Orc, who has a memory of pre-lapsarian times, insists that she must combine Female form with a garment which is truly divine. The 'Garment of God' is identifiable with Jerusalem, he observes. Bracher admirably sums up Orc's attitude: 'Why, asks Orc, is nature not pitying and compassionate in actuality, fulfilling individuals as God in eternity does in Jerusalem?' (1985: 94).

The words of Orc are performative: he exhorts the Shadowy Female to adopt a particular course of action. Her words might impress us as constative, but they actually have a clear illocutionary effect: they are a clear expression of her autonomy, serving to establish hers as a fully independent will which time and time again will no doubt provoke a response from Orc. There are no indications that peace between the two will ensue, and, amongst, other things, this has implications for Milton. In the poem, the focus will next shift to Rahab and Tirzah next. In her speech, the Shadowy Female connects the division of Rahab and Tirzah to her garment, and that division is instrumental in a possible seduction of Milton. Howard observes that

> The Shadowy Female outlines the method of perversion that the seductive Rahab and Tirzah attempt to put into practice. She is, in fact, the spiritual essence of Rahab and Tirzah. (1977: 222)

Hence, partly owing to her performed independence, which speaks to her unwillingness to yield to Orc, a threat to Milton is suggested.

Rahab and Tirzah

Subsequently, the focus shifts to Urizen. We gave this episode consideration in the Introduction and need not revisit it at this stage. Two characters observe Milton's struggle with Urizen on the banks of the Arnon: Rahab and Tirzah, mother and daughter. They have already been connected to Milton's family, and we also know of their first emergence, when Luetha gave birth to Death. In contrast to the Shadowy Female and Orc, the two address Milton directly.

The churches spoken of earlier are apposite here. Tirzah alludes to 'Three Heavens' in the speech we will turn to presently, but it is the twenty-seven that are being referenced. (These 'Three Heavens' are not to be confused with the three heavens of *Beulah*.) We saw that Milton's Shadow is spoken of not just in connection with the heavens and Churches, but also as 'A mournful form double; hermaphroditic: male & female/ In one wonderful body' (14.37–38, E108). Now we hear of three categories, comprising the 'Hermaphroditic', the 'Female-Males' and 'A Male within a Female'. The second grouping is identifiable with Tirzah; the third is identifiable with Rahab.

As Frye clarifies, in Blake's poetry, war is associated with men (for obvious reasons), natural religion is symbolically female (in so much poetry, nature is symbolically female), and natural religion is the cause of war. Hence, Rahab, identified as 'Religion hid in War' (37.43, E138), is a 'Male-Female' hermaphrodite figure. With respect to Tirzah (the 'Female-Male'), 'the man who is born in helpless dependence on an outward environment is a male imagination imprisoned within a female will' (2004: 301), as Frye succinctly puts it. Tirzah is a goddess of 'adaptation': the important self is the material self which matches the outward, material world. As we shall see, when Rahab and Tirzah speak, emphasis is placed upon the forming of human bodies (brain, heart and (male) loins) out of physical materials.

Milton's identity as a Mosaic figure is of great significance here. Like Moses, he goes as far as the river Jordan but must not pass over into the Promised Land. Of course Urizen is already stopping Milton's progress to Golgonooza, but Rahab and Tirzah would lead him astray as well. The illocutionary effect of their speech amounts to an elaborate invitation. They would have him abandon his work on Urizen, and they sing a song to tempt him across the river to Canaan. At the end of their speech, they call on him to reign there, as the King of Hazor did. Before that, they encourage him to enter 'Ephraim', the northern kingdom of Israel, denoted here through a reference to the main tribe of that region. Bloom observes that this suggestion is especially ironical, for the northern kingdom symbolizes 'the lost tribes and spiritual bondage' (1982: 917). But either way, entering that land would be a misstep. From Blake's point of view, the crossing of the river Jordan is not an entry into the Promised Land, but merely a journey to Canaan, which, as Frye explains, is 'the land possessed by a people who have given up the real Promised Land and settled down under the Mosaic law and the Levitical priesthood' (2005a: 255). Bloom suggests Blake concluded that Milton was wrong to support Cromwell's revolution, and that the temptation Milton resists here (despite his being offered a Cromwellian-type rule) obliquely references the temptation Milton yielded to in history (1982: 917).

The rhetorical strategy of Rahab and Tirzah is to promote their own involvement in human life, emphasizing their control of history, while expressing extreme scepticism about the most important figures in Milton's faith: Christ, Albion and Jerusalem. In an important way, their speech act is a sociopolitical performative: they speak from a position of what they think of as real temporal power, casting the powers that Milton invests in not as real and eternal but illusory and therefore impotent.

The two think they have a fighting chance of tempting Milton, partly, again, because his Puritanism was marked by a strong admixture of natural religion. In this world, they sing, it is Tirzah who triumphs: natural religion, here associated with Bacon ('experiments on Men'), is her religion, and war in Europe represents her work. Cruelty is 'holy'. They reference Orc and his captivity. They think of Orc only in terms of the outbreak of revolution, and, betraying a significant misunderstanding of Milton, attempt to convince him that no revolutions will occur in the land where he is king, assuring him that 'the fires of youth' remain bound with the 'Chain of jealousy'. The historical situation is described in terms of the Cambridge Milton had attended, London's 'dark-frowning towers', Europe beset by war, and with reference to the fates of the emanations of three zoas, Ahania (connected to Urizen), Enion (the emanation of Tharmas), and Vala (that of Luvah). Their demise is connected to Tirzah's triumph.

Proceeding with their discouraging, faith-sapping discourse, Rahab and Tirzah assure Milton that Christ will not come, and that Albion will never rouse himself from his slumbers. Tirzah is connected to Druidism: Christians 'are born for War! for Sacrifice to Tirzah!' They take an equally low view of Jerusalem: indeed, they suggest Jerusalem should also be offered up for sacrifice after a procession suggestive of mockery, like the one Shakespeare's Octavius Caesar plans for Cleopatra. Tirzah's is the associated with Hellenism; Jerusalem, a city symbolized by a woman, belongs to the Hebraic tradition. Tirzah suggests that Jerusalem's being brought to the place of sacrifice be celebrated by 'songs on the Grecian lyre'. Earlier, Blake had referred to the 'rocks of Horeb': having been given Biblical names, Milton's wives and daughters are pictured sitting around him like these rocks, and Milton's body is identified with the Rock Sinai. Now, clarifying the hopelessness of the situation, Albion's sons are spoken of in similar terms: the fourth, Scofield, named after the soldier who accused Blake of sedition, is a prisoner in armour. Hand, another son, is identified with 'a rock'; Hyle and Coban with 'Sinai & Horeb':

> The Man and Demon strove many periods. Rahab beheld
> Standing on Carmel; Rahab and Tirzah trembled to behold
> The enormous strife. one giving life, the other giving death
> To his adversary. and they sent forth all their sons & daughters
> In all their beauty to entice Milton across the river,
>
> The Twofold form Hermaphroditic: and the Double-sexed;
> The Female-male & the Male-female, self-dividing stood
> Before him in their beauty, & in cruelties of holiness!
> Shining in darkness, glorious upon the deeps of Entuthon.
>
> Saying. Come thou to Ephraim! behold the Kings of Canaan!
> The beautiful Amalekites, behold the fires of youth
> Bound with the Chain of jealousy by Los & Enitharmon;
> The banks of Cam: cold learnings streams: Londons dark-frowning towers;
> Lament upon the winds of Europe in Rephaims Vale.
> Because Ahania rent apart into a desolate night,
> Laments! & Enion wanders like a weeping inarticulate voice
> And Vala labours for her bread & water among the Furnaces
> Therefore bright Tirzah triumphs: putting on all beauty.
> And all perfection, in her cruel sports among the Victims,
> Come bring with thee Jerusalem with songs on the Grecian Lyre!
> In Natural Religion! in experiments on Men,
> Let her be Offerd up to Holiness! Tirzah numbers her;
> She numbers with her fingers every fibre ere it grow;
> Where is the Lamb of God? where is the promise of his coming?
> Her shadowy Sisters form the bones, even the bones of Horeb:
> Around the marrow! and the orbed scull around the brain!
> His Images are born for War! for Sacrifice to Tirzah!
> To Natural Religion! to Tirzah the Daughter of Rahab the Holy!
> She ties the knot of nervous fibres, into a white brain!
> She ties the knot of bloody veins, into a red hot heart!
> Within her bosom Albion lies embalmd, never to awake
> Hand is become a rock! Sinai & Horeb, is Hyle & Coban:
> Scofield is bound in iron armour before Reubens Gate!
> She ties the knot of milky seed into two lovely Heavens,
> Two yet but one: each in the other sweet reflected! these
> Are our Three Heavens beneath the shades of Beulah, land of rest!
> Come then to Ephraim & Manasseh O beloved-one!

Come to my ivory palaces O beloved of thy mother!
And let us bind thee in the bands of War & be thou King
Of Canaan and reign in Hazor where the Twelve Tribes meet.
(19.27–20.6, E113–114)

As we shall see at the start of the next chapter, Milton is not in the slightest won over by their invitation. Their speech may possess a certain amount of illocutionary force, but, ultimately it does not have the desired effect. Milton's redeemed self ignores it and continues his work, giving a human form ('life') to Urizen.

It will be impossible to proceed to Golgonooza in this context: he has in hands full with Urizen. But Milton will proceed to Golgonooza in another context, and, in one further context beyond that, he will defeat Satan by means of words, that triumph, as we shall see, impacting on his silent struggle with Urizen, and catalysing further restorative developments.

References

Blake, W. (1988), *The Complete Poetry and Prose of William Blake: Newly Revised Edition*, ed. D. V. Erdman, University of California Press: Berkeley.

Bloom, H., (1982), 'Commentary' in *The Complete Poetry and Prose of William Blake*, ed. D.V. Erdman, Berkeley: University of California Press, 894–972.

Bracher, M. (1985), *Being Form'd: Thinking Through Blake's Milton*, New York: Statin Hill Press.

Fox, S. (1976), *Poetic Form in Blake's Milton*, Princeton: Princeton University Press.

Frye, N. (2004), *Fearful Symmetry: A Study of William Blake*, ed. N. Halmi, Toronto: University of Toronto Press.

Frye, N. (2005a), *Northrop Frye on Milton and Blake*, ed. A. Esterhammer, Toronto: University of Toronto Press.

Howard, J. (1976), *Blake's Milton: A Study in Selfhood*, London: Associated University Presses.

4 Opposition to Milton in Golgonooza and Los's Defence of the 'Shadow Terrible'

After the events that we discussed in the previous chapter, the poem reaches a kind of impasse involving the three of these aspects of Milton's personality discussed at the start of the previous chapter: the redeemed self (struggling with Urizen), his body and his Humanity. Providing an account of the stage reached by the narrative, Blake again combines his schemata: Milton's redeemed self is identified with his 'spirit':

> ... Silent Milton stood before
> The darkend Urizen; as the sculptor silent stands before
> His forming image; he walks round it patient labouring.
> Thus Milton stood forming bright Urizen, while his Mortal part
> Sat frozen in the rock of Horeb: and his Redeemed portion,
> Thus form'd the Clay of Urizen; but within that portion
> His real Human walkd above in power and majesty
> Tho darkend; and the Seven Angels of the Presence attended him.
> (20.7-14, E114)

It makes sense to speak of these three aspects of Milton's self in the same breath because they are all suggestive of a process whereby his personality gets disaggregated. But the poem makes it clear that these parts do not add up to the whole of his personality. The reader of the poem has already heard of how, on another level, Milton – an apparently unitary Milton – becomes one with Blake. On one level, Milton's journey to Golgonooza is blocked by Urizen; but by virtue of his identity with Blake and their subsequent becoming one with Los, Milton may actually proceed to Golgonooza. We learn that

> ... travellers from Eternity. pass outward to Satans seat,
> But travellers to Eternity. pass inward to Golgonooza. (15.29–30, E111)

Blake may be travelling inwards, while Milton moves outwards, but they are joined as one as they journey to their destination. For this study, what is of special interest is that this character complex travels to Golgonooza and encounters verbal resistance, which necessitates language use, speeches, by Los. Here impactful performatives on the part of Los play a significant role, while the opponents fail in their attempt to stop Los, Blake and Milton. All the action is part of the instant, and also here the instant is secured.

Blake, Milton and Los: Context III

First, let's briefly consider the process whereby these characters unite with one another, focusing first on Blake and Milton. As already indicated, immediately prior to the section in which Milton is pictured with his wives and daughters, Blake tells us of Milton's appearing as a 'falling star' and of Milton's uniting with Blake:

> Then first I saw him in the Zenith as a falling star,
> Descending perpendicular, swift as the swallow or swift;
> And on my left foot falling on the tarsus, enterd there;
> But from my left foot a black cloud redounding spread over Europe. (15.47–50, E110)

We first see the star in the design on plate 1(3), and we can clearly see Milton as star entering Blake's left foot in the design of plate 14 and the black cloud 'redounding' in the design of plate 29. Bracher argues that the detaching of the cloud means that this process of identification results in a 'purification of the false elements of Milton's being' (1985: 85).

The narrative returns to Milton's uniting with Blake immediately after the description of the impasse spoken of a moment ago. Interestingly, we are told that that part of Milton, which may be identified as both Elect and Spectrous, detaches itself from Blake and seeks out Milton's mortal part, his body, over which, we learn, it will hover:

> For that portion namd the Elect: the Spectrous body of Milton:
> Redounding from my left foot into Los's Mundane space,
> Brooded over his Body in Horeb against the Resurrection
> Preparing it for the Great Consummation; red the Cherub on Sinai
> Glow'd; but in terrors folded round his clouds of blood. (20.20–24, E114)

Then, on plate 21, we hear of the union between Milton and Blake once again. Milton enters Blake's left foot, in what might seem a repetition of an earlier development:

> But Milton entering my Foot; I saw in the nether
> Regions of the Imagination; also all men on Earth,
> And all in Heaven, saw in the nether regions of the Imagination
> In Ulro beneath Beulah, the vast breach of Miltons descent.
> But I knew not that it was Milton, for man cannot know
> What passes in his members till periods of Space & Time
> Reveal the secrets of Eternity: for more extensive
> Than any other earthly things, are Mans earthly lineaments.
>
> And all this Vegetable World appeard on my left Foot,
> As a bright sandal formd immortal of precious stones & gold:
> I stooped down & bound it on to walk forward thro' Eternity.
> (21.4-14, E115)

Also of relevance is that later on plate 20, we learn how Milton's human portion is forcibly ejected from heaven. The Eternals react to Milton, specifically to that aspect of him which is like an Eighth Eye. Unaware of his true identity, they respond physically and violently:

> They rend the heavens round the Watchers in a fiery circle:
> And round the shadowy Eighth (20.46-47, E114)

This provokes a self-protecting response from the eight Eyes:

> ... the Eight close up the couch
> Into a tabernacle, and flee with cries down to the Deeps:
> Where Los opens his three wide gates, surrounded by raging fires
> They soon find their own place & join the Watchers of the Ulro
> (20.47-50, E114-115)

(It may be the 'Starry Ones' descending into Ulro in the upper right margin of the design of plate 21).

Los is also integrated into this composite identity. Prior to the second account of Milton's uniting with Blake, Los, in connection with the ejection of the Milton's Humanity along with the Seven Eyes of God (which brings him close to despair), experiences a crucial moment of insight: Milton may be the one to liberate Orc. It may be Milton who can do what he, Los, could not:

68 *Opposition to Milton*

> At last when desperation almost tore his heart in twain
> He recollected an old Prophecy in Eden recorded,
> And often sung to the loud harp at the immortal feasts
> That Milton of the Land of Albion should up ascend
> Forwards from Ulro from the Vale of Felpham; and set free
> Orc from his Chain of Jealousy (20.56–61, E115)

The focus shifts to Ololon (we shall consider this section at the beginning of chapter 5), before we learn of the unification of Blake-Milton with Los:

> While Los heard indistinct in fear, what time I bound my sandals
> On; to walk forward thro' Eternity, Los descended to me:
> And Los behind me stood; a terrible flaming Sun: just close
> Behind my back; I turned round in terror, and behold.
> Los stood in that fierce glowing fire; & he also stoop'd down
> And bound my sandals on in Udan-Adan; trembling I stood
> Exceedingly with fear & terror, standing in the Vale
> Of Lambeth: but he kissed me and wishd me health.
> And I became One Man with him arising in my strength:
> Twas too late now to recede. Los had enterd into my soul:
> His terrors now posses'd me whole! I arose in fury & strength.
> (22.4–14, E116–117)

(The moment when Los steps out of the sun to greet Blake is beautifully captured in the full-page design of plate 43(21).) It seems as though Blake-Milton began to walk through Eternity prior to their uniting with Los. But the journey is to be completed as Milton-Blake-Los.

In connection with Milton's re-entering the world through Blake, Frye speaks of Blake's employment of 'the Oriental myth of the Bodhisattva, the saint who voluntarily re-enters the world to help liberate it' (2005: 187). In connection with Blake's joining with Los, Cogan has written of how Blake describes something similar to 'New Testament representations of the *parousia*', 'a coming to be with' (2021: 186). Most interesting for the present purposes is how, to varying degrees, critics encourage us to see all these developments as iterations of a single experience. Howard suggests that 'Milton's human portion's entrance to Blake's foot and his joining the watchers are the same act' (1976: 231). But he views this twofold development as distinct from Milton's first joining with Blake. Fox, by contrast, concludes that the first and second joining of Milton with Blake are one and the same: 'in order to define this instantaneous process of descent

Blake ... [delineates] its beginning and its conclusion in two parallel passages' (1976: 88). In Fox's view, Milton's human portion, along with his spectre, unites with Blake, not during a second encounter, but in that single encounter. Adding the Bard's uniting with Milton to the 'series', Fox argues that all three unions are the ultimately the same event. We can discern 'three distinguishable stages, a series, it would seem, of subactions, but', she continues, 'Blake indicates repeatedly, by verbal echoes and by explicit references to the instant each event occurs, that the stages themselves are simultaneous' (1976: 60).

If we want to approach this element in the narrative biographically, we might simply observe that it corresponds to Blake's working productively with the legacy of Milton and evolving his own work. To fully understand this development, we must first comprehend that, for Blake, the poet, and the epic poet in particular, is of colossal social significance. The poet Shelley speaks of the poet's being 'the unacknowledged legislator of mankind', and Blake thinks of the poet as having perhaps an even more important role. Amongst other things, poetry provides us with a vision of apocalypse, as well as a sense of the powers precipitating a conclusion to history as well as those frustrating it. Crucially, a new poet may *hone* the work of a predecessor. Blake's *Milton* and *Jerusalem* and Milton's major works might strike us as utterly different, but from Blake's point of view his work represents an improvement on Milton's. And, for Blake, it is always the same figure who 'authors' these visions, Los, the fallen Urthona. Blake and Milton are both manifestations of that fallen zoa. He is their real identity and so, Milton and Blake having become one, they unite with Los.

Milton may proceed to Golgonooza in this other context. Now we will learn more about what is to be gained by proceeding to Golgonooza. Of course, it is bound up with apocalypse – when apocalypse will be, how (not) to bring it about, and what to do at this advanced stage of sacred history. But it is also a question of *seeing* Golgonooza in all its splendour.

Resistance I: Rintrah and Plamabron

As they journey to Golgonooza together, Los delivers a soliloquy. It is as though, through uniting with the two, he suddenly acquires a far more profound sense of self. An *anagnorisis* (a revelation of identity) is brought about by the union. It is also catalysed by the performative pronouncement through which he defines himself. He comments on his role as the keeper of all human acts which in fallen life disappear into the past without a trace. At least until apocalypse, all reality is permanent, and Los is in charge of its permanence. This charge he has is central to the idea which emerges through speech:

> I am that Shadowy Prophet who Six Thousand Years ago
> Fell from my station in the Eternal bosom. Six Thousand Years
> Are finishd. I return! both Time & Space obey my will.
> I in Six Thousand Years walk up and down: for not one Moment
> Of Time is lost, nor one Event of Space unpermanent
> But all remain: every fabric of Six Thousand Years
> Remains permanent: tho' on the Earth where Satan
> Fell, and was cut off all things vanish & are seen no more
> They vanish not from me & mine, we guard them first & last
> The generations of men run on in the tide of Time
> But leave their destind lineaments permanent for ever & ever.
> (22.15–25, E117)

Towards the end of the journey, this character complex is met with resistance, all of it verbal. The first line of resistance is Rintrah and Palamabron, Los's sons, whom we also know from the Bard's Song. Rintrah and Palamabron meet Los at the 'Gate of Golgonooza' (M22:27, E117). Despite the fact that it is a character complex, they encounter, it is the Miltonic dimension they focus on, although they refer to Blake's left foot as well. Los agrees with much of what they say, but his insight is greater than theirs. As Fox points out, even though Milton's Shadow redounds from Milton-Blake when Milton enters Blake's left foot, Los's sons still see Blake's foot as 'black', suggesting an inferior understanding of the situation (1976: 98). Their focus shifts only momentarily when they address Albion directly in a performative which aims to rouse him. The illocutionary force of their different arguments is clear: they insist that Milton-Blake must be treated as an antagonist. Specifically, they argue for the need to commit Milton-Blake to the furnaces named Bowlahoola. The connection between Milton's creed and war, explored in the second chapter, structures the thinking here as well. In their eyes, Milton bears the responsibility for contemporary warfare and possible intensifications of it.

The two begin by expressing alarm about Los's being determined to protect Milton. They know he has chosen to 'refuse/ To throw him into the furnaces', and they fear Milton will liberate Orc and unleash a train of demonic figures, including Satan, on Albion. They direct Los's attention first to Blake's left foot (where Blake was joined by Milton) and second to the Shadowy Female (whom we came across earlier) and the daughters of Los, all of whom are also troubled by the arrival of

Milton. Rintrah and Palamabron associate 'a new religion' with the response of the Daughters of Los to Milton. They speak in the manner of historians of religion and civilization. Once again, it is Milton's Puritanism which is a cause for concern. The two have a sense that the end of history, again iterated through the notion of 'Churches', has been approached, and that, in response, Rahab and Tirzah have produced deism. Milton is implicated because his religion leads to the deism of Voltaire and Rousseau, through whom Rahab and Tirzah have done their work. War on the continent is the direct result of the thought of the two French thinkers.

Swedenborg's work has also been systematically 'perverted' by Rahab and Tirzah. Swedenborg was a major influence on the thinking of Blake, but since *The Marriage of Heaven and Hell* Blake had been a trenchant critic of the Swedish mystic. Here his work is spoken of in connection with the decline in religion associated with eighteenth-century French thought, as well as the Hellenism we have already touched on a number of times. That he is hailed as the 'strongest of men, the Samson shorn by the Churches' might create the impression that Rintrah and Palamabron wish to eulogize him, but their intention is to offer a critique. Blake had provided a disquisition on the marriage of heaven and hell. Swedenborg's chief error is represented by his idea of a separable heaven and hell, Rintrah and Palamabron essentially seeing Swedenborg as Blake does.

These developments in religious thought catalyse a historical period which Blake describes using the imagery of Revelation. He throws the emphasis onto a figure referred to as 'Mystery', easily recognizable as the Great Whore. (In Revelation, one of seven angels takes John to see a figure who sits upon 'a scarlet coloured beast', and he sees, written on her forehead, the name 'Mystery, Babylon the Great, the Mother of Harlots and abominations of the earth' (Revelation, 17: 59).) The imagery refers to times of war on both sides of the Atlantic. Blake's condensed vision involves two brides (Jerusalem and Mystery). Frye comments that Mystery is 'the ultimate form of nature or the "female will"' (2004: 143). In the second chapter, we commented on the mysterious nature of *femme fatale* figures representing fallen nature. For Blake, the unfallen world is merely concealed, and what it is concealed by is the fallen world: the Great Whore, fallen nature, is called Mystery because her existence obscures the vision of the unfallen world. 'Apocalypse means revelation', observes Frye, 'and the Great Whore is the chief thing revelation comes to remove, which is Mystery' (2004: 143). The other bride, Jerusalem, is the unfallen world; consequently, her persecution (spoken of in this passage) may point to the conditions of fallen existence, and therefore concealment again.

Suddenly emerging as a sole speaker, Rintrah speaks of an eleventh-hour resistance: Westley and Whitefield are representatives of English Methodism, for which Blake has a great deal of sympathy, and it is viewed as the binary opposite of the deism associated with Rousseau and Voltaire. But England has not embraced the thinking of the two miraculous thinkers. Again voicing Blake's ideas, Rintrah speaks of the faithlessness of the times heralded by Voltaire and Rousseau. It is as though Westley and Whitefield had met the fate of Elijah and Moses, the 'Witnesses' of Revelation, described in that book: 'The Witnesses lie dead in the Street of the Great City' (Revelation, 11:8). Imitating their voices, Rintrah mocks deists, who dismiss miracles, and insists that the great Methodists *were* miracles.

As though turning away from Los for a moment, Rintrah directs his speech to the slumbering Albion. Switching to a different performative focus, he tries to wake the giant, painting a picture of the current historical scene. (Again, there is evidence of the simultaneity of everything happening in the poem. Albion stirs in his sleep and hears the terrible sounds of war. But, as Fox persuasively suggests (1976: 100), this is merely another iteration of the moment earlier in the poem when 'Albion's Humanity began to turn upon his Couch' (20.25, E114), apparently a reaction to Milton's descent). Rintrah speaks very much in the manner of Blake's earlier self – the younger poet and painter who, like his contemporaries, believed that the revolutionary age was ushering in apocalypse. The end of history is upon them, says Rintrah. There have already been two blasts of the trumpet – the American and French Revolutions. It is time for Albion to rouse himself, but he tarries. Meanwhile, however, 'the Covering Cherub advances from the East': Bloom argues that this represents 'the terror of continental warfare' (1982: 919).

Milton will 'consume' both Los and his sons, argues Rintrah. For the first time, it is suggested that Milton's Shadow, identifiable with the twenty-seven churches, and both Rahab and Tirzah, is also identifiable with the Covering Cherub. Aware of the identification of Milton's Shadow with the Covering Cherub (but unaware that there is more to Milton), Rintrah states that Milton has entered into the Covering Cherub and goes on to speak of how he has also become one with Albion's sons and daughters. Gwendolen and Conwenna, last and first of Albion's daughters, are another female-will complex, and they are identified as another garment image: a 'garment woven/ Of War & Religion' adorning Milton.

Opposition to Milton 73

Ending where they began, they see that the only option is to throw Milton-Blake into the furnaces named Bowlahoola, the illocutionary force of their whole speech tending towards dealing with Milton in this way:

> Rintrah and Palamabron met us at the Gate of Golgonooza
> Clouded with discontent. & brooding in their minds terrible things
> They said. O Father most beloved! O merciful Parent!
> Pitying and permitting evil, tho strong & mighty to destroy.
> Whence is this Shadow terrible? wherefore dost thou refuse
> To throw him into the Furnaces! knowest thou not that he
> Will unchain Orc? & let loose Satan, Og, Sihon & Anak,
> Upon the Body of Albion? for this he is come! behold it written
> Upon his fibrous left Foot black! most dismal to our eyes
> The Shadowy Female shudders thro' heaven in torment inexpressible!
> And all the Daughters of Los prophetic wail: yet in deceit,
> They weave a new Religion from new Jealousy of Theotormon!
> Miltons Religion is the cause: there is no end to destruction!
> Seeing the Churches at their Period in terror & despair:
> Rahab created Voltaire; Tirzah created Rousseau;
> Asserting the Self-righteousness against the Universal Saviour,
> Mocking the Confessors & Martyrs, claiming Self-righteousness;
> With cruel Virtue: making War upon the Lambs Redeemed;
> To perpetuate War & Glory. to perpetuate the Laws of Sin:
> They perverted Swedenborgs Visions in Beulah & in Ulro;
> To destroy Jerusalem as a Harlot & her Sons as Reprobates;
> To raise up Mystery the Virgin Harlot Mother of War,
> Babylon the Great, the Abomination of Desolation!
> O Swedenborg! strongest of men, the Samson shorn by the Churches!
> Shewing the Transgresors in Hell, the proud Warriors in Heaven:
> Heaven as a Punisher & Hell as One under Punishment:
> With Laws from Plato & his Greeks to renew the Trojan Gods,
> In Albion; & to deny the value of the Saviours blood.
> But then I rais'd up Whitefield, Palamabron raisd up Westley,
> And these are the cries of the Churches before the two Witnesses
> Faith in God the dear Saviour who took on the likeness of men:
> Becoming obedient to death, even the death of the Cross
> The Witnesses lie dead in the Street of the Great City
> No Faith is in all the Earth: the Book of God is trodden under Foot:

> He sent his two Servants Whitefield & Westley; were they Prophets
> Or were they Idiots or Madmen? shew us Miracles!
> Can you have greater Miracles than these? Men who devote
> Their lifes whole comfort to intire scorn & injury & death
> Awake thou sleeper on the Rock of Eternity Albion awake
> The trumpet of Judgment hath twice sounded: all Nations are awake
> But thou art still heavy and dull: Awake Albion awake!
> Lo Orc arises on the Atlantic. Lo his blood and fire
> Glow on Americas shore: Albion turns upon his Couch
> He listens to the sounds of War, astonishd and confounded:
> He weeps into the Atlantic deep, yet still in dismal dreams
> Unwakend! and the Covering Cherub advances from the East:
> How long shall we lay dead in the Street of the great City
> How long beneath the Covering Cherub give our Emanations
> Milton will utterly consume us & thee our beloved Father
> He hath enterd into the Covering Cherub, becoming one with
> Albions dread Sons, Hand, Hyle & Coban surround him as
> A girdle; Gwendolen & Conwenna as a garment woven
> Of War & Religion; let us descend & bring him chained
> To Bowlahoola O father most beloved! O mild Parent!
> Cruel in thy mildness, pitying and permitting evil
> Tho strong and mighty to destroy, O Los our beloved Father!
> (22.27–23.20, E117-118)

The manifold illocutionary force is clear enough, but it yields little in terms of the kind of reaction they want from Los. The main perlocutionary effect is a defiant verbal response on the part of Los. Los remains the father of Rintrah and Palambron, and therefore a patriarchal authority figure, but the insight he has had about Milton reinvents his role, turning him into a figure espousing something close to the opposite of what he (no doubt) authoritatively advanced before he understood the significance of Milton's return. He only explicitly offers resistance to the desire of his sons to throw Milton into Bowlahoola at the end of his speech. Prior to that, through performative language he repeatedly urges patience: patience is the key to apocalypse, he insists. Importantly, Rintrah and Palamabron have spoken of revolution and apocalypse with authority. But Los has gone beyond that understanding of how apocalypse will begin: even if the two great Revolutions suggest a completion of the seventh cycle, it is wrong to try to *precipitate* apocalypse at this time. It may be that Rintrah and Palambron are impatient for the Eighth Eye or

Second Coming. But Los knows that they would only perpetuate history, not bring it to its 'comedic' conclusion. Then, again in performative discourse, he pleads with his sons: he throws the emphasis onto his sons' *remaining with* him, in contrast to the other sons, who, at great cost, left him. Of course, performatively, the point of the whole speech is also to enlighten. Rintrah and Palamabron stubbornly resist its light, as it were, but Los's speech *is* enlightening, and so it qualifies as performative or illocutionary on that level, too.

Los begins by sharing with his sons his insight about the return of the Elect Milton, returning to the imagery of Orc and the 'Chain/ Of jealousy'. Importantly, Los already knows that Milton will free Orc in different circumstances from the ones they find themselves in – he will rise up from Felpham, which, as we shall see, is where Blake is writing *Milton*. (The exact meaning of Los's understanding of the prophecy is unclear, but we may be able to cast some light on it at the very end of this commentary.)

In connection with this knowledge of Milton's role, Los, for a second time – he also begins his speech with the need for patience – urges his sons to be patient at this advanced stage of sacred history. He then makes a brief reference to the Females who are the antagonists of Satan and his 'watch-fiends'. Mankind leads a double life: it exists as spectres before Satan's Bar, and as vegetations in Generation. The Watch-Fiends record every transgression ('Human loves/ And graces'), but the Females are capable of concealing loves and graces from Satan's henchmen.

Employing the traditional apocalyptic imagery of harvest and vintage, Los imitates the voice of those who long for apocalypse, before responding to their call. He provides a history of premature action and which had disastrous consequences, especially religious polarization. Adding to the performative texture of his speech, he issues a mandate, 'Let it not be so now!', disavowing religious wars, even if it might appear that they are part of the process whereby apocalypse is catalysed. Crucially, he and his sons have been placed in Golgonooza by the 'Universal Brotherhood & Mercy', and they have been equipped with 'powers fitted to circumscribe this dark Satanic death/ ... that the Seven Eyes of God may have space for Redemption'. Earlier, Los suggested that he may be in charge of an accumulative process whereby a structure in time gets completed, which suggests steady progress to apocalypse. Now he admits to uncertainty about how apocalypse will *finally* be set in motion. They simply must wait for Albion, also the Eighth Eye, to awaken. If agency is instrumental in the onset of resurrection and apocalypse, paradoxically, it is because of the decision on the part of the agent to be patient.

Urging patience for a third time, Los states that certain factors point to the immanence of apocalypse: the six thousand years of history are coming to an end, and Milton's descent reliably indicates that mankind is on the cusp of restoration. Los says that Milton is 'of the Elect' – Milton is still easily identifiable as one who, as a member of the Elect, took up his place in 'heaven'. No member of the Elect has ever returned from Eden, and this unprecedented development is a reliable sign of apocalypse. Yet again, Los then urges the sons to be patient.

Shifting the focus of his rhetoric, Los then exhorts his remaining four sons not to leave him. Twelve have already departed. They left him at the time of the events of the Bard's Song, which is spoken of as lasting a thousand years (the thousand years preceding the six thousand of human history). The sons of Los have the names of the sons of Israel. In other poems, Blake lists twelve sons of Israel, and Los is no doubt speaking of the flight of all twelve even if only seven are named. (Manazzoth and Menassheh are the same son. The two names are different transliterations of the same Biblical name, which carry different meanings. See Damon, 1988: 261.) Los explains that by leaving him, they fell under the power of Tirzah.

Imploring them for a second time not to leave him, Los names his four remaining sons. He continues his exhortation by addressing his sons individually in highly rhetorical terms, alluding to two emblematic moments in the history of the Fall. In the earlier *The Four Zoas*, the daughters of Amalek, Canaan and Moab are spoken of in connection with Rahab and Tirzah (109:28, E378). Los asks Rintrah if he remembers how the three fell down to the state in which they became nations. Employing the story of Joseph and his brothers as another narrative of Fall (and producing a particular variation on the story in which Joseph is sold to the Amalekite after being 'wrapd in needle-work/ Of emblematic texture'), Los asks Palamabron if he remembers how Joseph was taken to Egypt.

Los then spells out the implications of his sons' leaving him. Aware of how on another plane Milton is in Ulro, he warns them that if they follow Milton, they will become 'poor mortal vegetations/ Beneath the moon of Ulro'. Using the verb (unusually) in an imperative, Los demands his sons *pity* him.

Los also wishes to provide a narrative for the present situation of the world, where the four Christian churches, which complete sacred history (the history of the twenty-seven churches), are pictured 'Stretchd over Europe & Asia'. He turns to the figure of Lazarus, raised from the dead by Christ, but here the emphasis is on the misuse of the miracle, which results in the false churches. He then turns to a figure invoked by his sons: the Covering Cherub. Identifying Lazarus with 'the Vehicular Body of Albion', and the Covering Cherub with the 'Spectre of Albion', Los tells his sons how he witnessed the former rise into the latter, when Christ raised Lazarus from the dead, whereupon the Covering Cherub took on the form of the four Christian churches of Blake's sacred history. Referring to the Body of Albion rising into the Covering Cherub, Damon expertly observes 'Understood literally by man's reason ("the Spectre of Albion") as the resurrection of the physical (not spiritual body), the miracle became part of the false doctrine of the church ("the Covering Cherub")' (1988: 236).

Urging his sons to devote their energies to overcoming Eternal Death, Los then turns to the roles of 'Cathedrons Looms', Bowlahoola and Allamanda, features of Golgonooza which this commentary will turn to presently. He reminds them that Human Form is superior to the 'Fibrous Vegetation' mankind is reduced to in its Polypus state. Cathedron, associated with Enitharmon's daughters, appears genuinely productive, but endeavours carried out there may also be perceived negatively.[1] Viewing the process from a higher viewpoint, now Los emphasizes that 'Cathedrons Looms weave only Death/A Web of Death'. As Damon surmises, 'From the higher point of view ... the looms "weave only death" from Eternity' (1988: 74). Returning to the main point of Rintrah and Palamabron, and rejecting their favoured course of action, Los argues that, while those who do not belong to the Elect may be thrown into Bowlahoola, where they will assume Human Form, Milton must not be treated in this way. Just as Satan, though guilty, could not be condemned, so the sons must not cast Milton's Elect self into Bowlahoola. As an 'Elected form', he is different from 'the Vegetated Mortals'. Again: he is an unequivocal sign of immanent apocalypse:

And Los thus spoke. O noble Sons, be patient yet a little
I have embracd the falling Death, he is become One with me
O Sons we live not by wrath. by mercy alone we live!
I recollect an old Prophecy in Eden recorded in gold; and oft
Sung to the harp: That Milton of the land of Albion.
Should up ascend forward from Felphams Vale & break the Chain
Of jealousy from all its roots; be patient therefore O my Sons
These lovely Females form sweet night and silence and secret
Obscurities to hide from Satans Watch-Fiends. Human loves
And graces; lest they write them in their Books, & in the Scroll
Of mortal life, to condemn the accused: who at Satans Bar

Tremble in Spectrous Bodies continually day and night
While on the Earth they live in sorrowful Vegetations
O when shall we tread our Wine-presses in heaven; and Reap
Our wheat with shoutings of joy, and leave the Earth in peace
Remember how Calvin and Luther in fury premature
Sow'd War and stern division between Papists & Protestants
Let it not be so now! O go not forth in Martyrdoms & Wars
We were plac'd here by the Universal Brotherhood & Mercy
With powers fitted to circumscribe this dark Satanic death
And that the Seven Eyes of God may have space for Redemption.
But how this is as yet we know not, and we cannot know;
Till Albion is arisen; then patient wait a little while,
Six Thousand years are passd away the end approaches fast;
This mighty one is come from Eden, he is of the Elect,
Who died from Earth & he is returnd before the Judgment. This thing
Was never known that one of the holy dead should willing return
Then patient wait a little while till the Last Vintage is over:
Till we have quenchd the Sun of Salah in the Lake of Udan Adan
O my dear Sons! leave not your Father, as your brethren left me[.]
Twelve Sons successive fled away in that thousand years of sorrow
Of Palamabrons Harrow, & of Rintrahs wrath & fury:
Reuben & Manazzoth & Gad & Simeon & Levi,
And Ephraim & Judah were Generated, because
They left me, wandering with Tirzah: Enitharmon wept
One thousand years, and all the Earth was in a watry deluge
We calld him Menasseh because of the Generations of Tirzah
Because of Satan: & the Seven Eyes of God continually
Guard round them, but I the Fourth Zoa am also set
The Watchman of Eternity, the Three are not! & I am preserved
Still my four mighty ones are left to me in Golgonooza
Still Rintrah fierce, and Palamabron mild & piteous
Theotormon filld with care, Bromion loving Science
You O my Sons still guard round Los. O wander not & leave me
Rintrah, thou well rememberest when Amalek & Canaan
Fled with their Sister Moab into the abhorred Void
They became Nations in our sight beneath the hands of Tirzah.
And Palamabron thou rememberest when Joseph an infant;
Stolen from his nurses cradle wrapd in needle-work
Of emblematic texture, was sold to the Amalekite,
Who carried him down into Egypt where Ephraim & Menasseh
Gatherd my Sons together in the Sands of Midian
And if you also flee away and leave your Fathers side,

Opposition to Milton 79

> Following Milton into Ulro, altho your power is great
> Surely you also shall become poor mortal vegetations
> Beneath the Moon of Ulro: pity then your Fathers tears
> When Jesus raisd Lazarus from the Grave I stood & saw
> Lazarus who is the Vehicular Body of Albion the Redeemd
> Arise into the Covering Cherub who is the Spectre of Albion
> By martyrdoms to suffer: to watch over the Sleeping Body.
> Upon his Rock beneath his Tomb. I saw the Covering Cherub
> Divide Four-fold into Four Churches when Lazarus arose
> Paul, Constantine, Charlemaine, Luther; behold they stand before us
> Stretchd over Europe & Asia. come O Sons, come, come away
> Arise O Sons give all your strength against Eternal Death
> Lest we are vegetated, for Cathedrons Looms weave only Death
> A Web of Death: & were it not for Bowlahoola & Allamanda
> No Human Form but only a Fibrous Vegetation
> A Polypus of soft affections without Thought or Vision
> Must tremble in the Heavens & Earths thro all the Ulro space[.]
> Throw all the Vegetated Mortals into Bowlahoola
> But as to this Elected Form who is returnd again
> He is the Signal that the Last Vintage now approaches
> Nor Vegetation may go on till all the Earth is reapd (23.32-24.43,
> E119-120)

Los's speech fails to achieve everything that he hoped for, but it achieves enough. Interestingly, we learn that the sons are unconvinced of his account of history and how to deal with Milton; they apparently cannot stop Los – or take Milton to Bowlahoola, but they register their discontent, and they remain, we learn, in a cycle of contestation (24:44-47, E120). But the 'progress' of Los and Milton is secured by Los's speech: they continue their journey to Golgonooza, Bowlahoola and Allamanda heaving into view shortly after the agonistic exchange with Rintrah and Palamabron. That progress counts as the most significant perlocutionary effect of Los's speech.

Golgonooza I: Context IV

We need to consider one further cluster of speeches, delivered in Bowlahoola. Before turning to that speech cluster, we might pause to consider how Blake describes Golgonooza (of which Bowlahoola is a part) in Book I.

We learned of how Los starts to build Golgonooza at a fairly early stage of the Fall. Comprising Allamanda and Bowlahoola, as well as

80 Opposition to Milton

Golgonooza itself, it is a country and a city in the spiritual world, the world as it is seen by the imagination. It is the 'spiritual fourfold London' (20.40, E114), and it is placed in 'the loins of Albion' (ibid.), though in another description London is between his knees (39.39, E141), or 'in the midst' of the universe of fallen zoas (19:24, E113).

Its location is also tied in with the figure of Satan. Blake urges readers not to look to the sky in search of a sky-father. But our inner worlds, the way to Golgonooza, are actually guarded by two figures named Og and Anak (Biblical giants), and the gates to Golgonoooza are behind Satan's seat:

> Seek not thy heavenly father then beyond the skies:
> There Chaos dwells & ancient Night & Og & Anak old:
> For every human heart has gates of brass & bars of adamant,
> Which few dare unbar because dread Og & Anak guard the gates
> Terrific! and each mortal brain is walld and moated round
> Within: and Og & Anak watch here; here is the Seat
> Of Satan in its Webs; for in brain and heart and loins
> Gates open behind Satans Seat to the City of Golgonooza
> Which is the spiritual fourfold London, in the loins of Albion
> (20.32–40, E114)

Bowlahoola is Los's forge in the centre of Golgonooza, where the sons of Los carry out their work; Allamanda is 'the Cultivated land/ Around the City of Golgonooza' (27.43, E125). In one description, the 'Forests of Entuthon' (27.42, E125) surround Allamanda; in another account, Entuthon is to the east of Golgonooza – in this description it contains the Lake of Udan-Adan (26:25, E123). The Wine-press, where the sons of Luvah toil, is 'eastward of Golgonooza, before the Seat/ of Satan' (27.1, E124). The mills of Theotormon – another of Los's sons – are on the edge of the lake, and associated with the element of water. Luban and Cathedron are not given locations in *Milton*, but in *Jerusalem*, Luban is associated with the North Gate of Golgonooza, and Cathedron is to be found in that gate.

In *Milton*, the zoas, and more importantly their sons and daughters, are associated with activities carried out in these different areas of Golgonooza. Mainly, it is the children of Los and Enitharmon who are spoken of. (We'll turn to the sons of Luvah and the Wine-press in the next section.) Because the Gate of the Tongue is closed, Tharmas has no role, and, although Urizen's sons' work is alluded to, little is made of their endeavours by Blake.

A number of Los's sons take care of 'Souls' as they take on or leave bodies. Blake scholars suggest that Blake employs the imagery of Homer's Cave of the Nymphs here. In the *Odyssey*, the northern gate is for mortals, whereas the southern is for gods. In *Milton*, the gates are associated with mortals receiving their bodies (the northern) and leaving them (the southern), and they are identified with British locations:

> There are Two Gates thro which all Souls descend. One Southward
> From Dover Cliff to Lizard Point. the other toward the North
> Caithness & rocky Durness, Pentland & John Groats House.
>
> The Souls descending to the Body, wail on the right hand
> Of Los; & those deliverd from the Body, on the left hand (26.13-17, E123)

(See the design of plate 25 (26) for Blake's depiction of the gates as the cliff faces of the north and south of Britain.)

We already know that, as Los says,

> were it not for Bowlahoola & Allamanda
> No Human Form but only a Fibrous Vegetation
> A Polypus of soft affections without Thought or Vision
> Must tremble in the Heavens & Earths thro all the Ulro space[.]
> (24.36–39, E120)

In one passage, Blake provides an account of how different sons have specific tasks. He speaks of how some sons provide form for 'Passions' (28.1, E125) and 'Doubts & fears unform'd & wretched & melancholy' (28.9, E125) – 'porches of iron & silver' (28.1, E125) for the former, 'Cabinets richly fabricate of gold & ivory' (28.8, E125) for the latter. Then the work of specific sons becomes the focus. We learn of Antamon's drawing outlines with his 'golden pen' (28.17, E126) for spectres, the tricks used by Theotormon and Sotha to get spectres to adopt form, how the sons of Ozoth (associated with the Optic Nerve) deprive the materially minded of sight, while enriching the 'the poor indigent' (28.36, E126), and eventually we learn of how Rintrah and Palamabron 'govern over Day & Night/In Allamanda & Entuthon Benython where souls wail' (29.27–28, E127). Importantly, Blake foregrounds the fact that it is in Bowlahoola that souls acquire their group status, elect, reprobate or redeemed. Spectres are inclined to particular classes before they even have bodies:

> For the various Classes of Men are all markd out determinate
> In Bowlahoola; & as the Spectres choose their affinities
> So they are born on Earth, & every Class is determinate (26.37–39, E123–124)

Enitharmon's daughters also have a role in the creation of bodies, associated with Cathedron, which appears genuinely productive:

> And every Generated Body in its inward form,
> Is a garden of delight & a building of magnificence,
> Built by the Sons of Los in Bowlahoola & Allamanda
> And the herbs & flowers & furniture & beds & chambers
> Continually woven in the Looms of Enitharmons Daughters
> In bright Cathedrons golden Dome with care & love & tears (26.31–36, E123)

The work of Enithamron's daughters seems to compliment that of Los's sons. At the end, the work of Enitharmon and her daughters appears entirely benevolent, when contrasted with that of Tirzah:

> But Enitharmon and her Daughters take the pleasant charge.
> To give them to their lovely heavens till the Great Judgment Day
> Such is their lovely charge. But Rahab & Tirzah pervert
> Their mild influences, therefore the Seven Eyes of God walk round
> The Three Heavens of Ulro, where Tirzah & her Sisters
> Weave the black Woof of Death upon Entuthon Benython
> In the Vale of Surrey where Horeb terminates in Rephaim (29.51–57, E128)

The necessary caveat is that, as already discussed, Los, seeing things from the point of view of Eternity, states that 'Cathedrons Looms weave only Death' (24.35, E120), which, by implication, suggests an ambiguity inherent in the work of Enitharmon.

In another respect, Los's sons are in charge of time and space. They transform the external world just as they provide spectres with bodies. Abstract understandings of time and space parallel the naked life of the spectres, and the sons of Los give them 'bodies'. His sons build all the conventional times periods – minutes, seconds and so on – but they are identifiable with a range of things: tents, gates, walls, terraces, barriers, bridges and flaming fire. Space is also reconceived:

Opposition to Milton 83

The Sky is an immortal tent built by the Sons of Los
And every Space that a Man views around his dwelling-place:
Standing on his own roof, or in his garden on a mount
Of twenty-five cubits in height, such space is his Universe;
And on its verge the Sun rises & sets. the Clouds bow
To meet the flat Earth & the Sea in such an orderd Space:
The Starry heavens reach no further but here bend and set
On all sides & the two Poles turn on their valves of gold:
And if he move his dwelling-place, his heavens also move.
Wher'eer he goes & all his neighbourhood bewail his loss:
Such are the Spaces called Earth & such its dimension: (29.4-14, E127)

Where he simply provides his favoured account of time when discussing that dimension, here Blake attacks the modern scientist's understanding of space, claiming that it alters 'The ratio of the Spectators organs' (29.18, E127). Dismissing the fantasy of 'a Globe rolling thro Voidness' (29.16, E127), he insists on space as the world which a person sees all around them.

The descriptions of time and space reach parallel conclusions. Blake structures his thinking around 'pulsations' or 'Moments', on the one hand, and the 'red globule' in a human body, on the other, emblematizing time and space, respectively. Up to a point, his interest is in the 'moment'. 'A Moment equals a pulsation of the artery' (28.47, E126), we learn. Every moment also has a 'couch of Gold for soft repose' (28.46, E126). As we shall see, Blake is especially interested in 'a Moment in each day that Satan cannot find' (35.42, E136). But his focus is also on the unit of time which is *less than* a pulsation of the artery or 'Moment'. We are also told that 'between every two Moments stands a Daughter of Beulah' (28.48, E126), and, more importantly, that just as eternity is manifest in an hour, so all of human history is equal to a division of time which is less than a pulsation:

Every Time less than a pulsation of the artery
Is equal in its period to Six Thousand Years
For in this Period the Poets Work is Done (28.63-29.2, E127)

Similarly, while a space larger than a globule is 'visionary', everything smaller than a globule is, like the 'Wild Flower', a gateway to eternity:

For every Space larger than a Globule of Mans blood.
Is visionary: and is created by the Hammer of Los

And every Space smaller than a Globule of Mans blood. opens
Into Eternity of which this vegetable Earth is but a shadow. (29.
19–22, E127)

To turn last of all to the activities of Los himself, towards the end of Book I, Blake rehearses a version of the Fall focused on the senses of Man. He supplements that account with a vision of Los's restorative activities 'in the Nerves of the Ear', mentioning Tharmas in passing:

And in the Nerves of the Ear, (for the Nerves of the Tongue are closed)
On Albions Rock Los stands creating the glorious Sun each morning
And when unwearied in the evening he creates the Moon
Death to delude, who all in terror at their splendor leaves
His prey while Los appoints, & Rintrah & Palamabron guide
The Souls clear from the Rock of Death, that Death himself may wake
In his appointed season when the ends of heaven meet.
Then Los conducts the Spirits to be Vegetated, into
Great Golgonooza, free from the four iron pillars of Satans Throne
(Temperance, Prudence, justice, Fortitude, the four pillars of tyranny)
That Satans Watch-Fiends touch them not before they Vegetate.
(29.40–50, E128)

Golgonooza, however, is a more fully integrated place than we have yet done justice to. Tied in with the fact that the Fall takes place in a single body, Golgonooza may be thought of in connection with Albion's body; in addition, Golgonooza, a city, is identifiable with Albion's emanation, Jerusalem. Then again, Los is 'the builder of the eternal form of human civilization, and [...] therefore a smith, a worker in metal and fire, the two great instruments of civilized life' (Frye 2004: 250), and we should think of Golgonooza as human civilization approaching its completion in time. Speaking of the connection between Golgonooza and Blake's world, Frye observes that 'A worldwide commercial unity seems to be emerging from national rivalries; and science evolves an increasingly coherent form out of knowledge, as law does out of conflict. Commerce, science, and law in Blake's day seem to be proceeding to some kind of historical finality' (2004: 258). The dimensions of Golgonooza, then, are identifiable with *aspects* of civilization.

Opposition to Milton 85

Consequently, Blake speaks aspects of Golgonooza, the body and civilization all in one breath. So, Allamanda, symbol for 'Commerce,' is 'Cultivated Land/Around the city of Golgonooza' (27.42, E125), but also the nervous system in the body (Damon, 1988: 17) or the heart (Frye, 2004: 258). Bowlahoola, the forge and furnace, is Law, but also the stomach, as well as the heart and lungs – its Bellows, Hammers and Furnaces are identified with the Animal Lungs, Animal Heart and Stomach, respectively. Together, they also represent science: 'Science is divided into Bowlahoola & Allamanda' (27.63, E125). Golgonooza is a combination of Allamanda and Bowlahoola, but also something in its own right. It represents 'Art & Manufacture' (24.50, E120), and it may be associated with the brain. It is also the voluntary realm of the body emerging in time, in contrast to the involuntary functions. And it may emerge fully only when Allamanda and Bowlahoola are complete. 'Once the heart and stomach of a larger human body appear', observes Frye, 'a larger human brain will soon follow them, and the Golden Age of Atlantis, when "all had originally one language, and one religion", will be restored' (2004: 331–332).

Resistance II: the Sons of Luvah

Fox sums up what has happened with great precision, emphasizing the simultaneity of everything:

> the appearance of the Bard within Milton is his decision to descend; the decision is the descent; the descent is the merger with Blake; Milton's merger with Blake is Los's merger with Blake. Each of these phases of the pivotal action, Milton's descent through the vortex, is a momentous decision occasioned both by fear and by faith in prophetic truth; consequently each is represented in terms of the conflicts that produce it: the Bard's feud with the eternals, the Zoas' strife with their emanations, Milton's battles with spectre and emanation, Los's argument with his sons. (1976: 105)

All the acts in the poem are facets of a single act, and all the speeches have been aspects of it's repetition that single act, which is largely verbal.

There is one more speech cluster to the add to the complex of speeches. Los's next speech (to the sons of Luvah) is preceded by two short speeches on the part of the sons. The sons are connected with the Wine-press in Golgonooza, but also associated with the Rhine:

86 *Opposition to Milton*

> The Wine-press on the Rhine groans loud, but all its central beams
> Act more terrific in the central Cities of the Nations
> Where Human Thought is crushd beneath the iron hand of Power.
> There Los puts all into the Press, the Opressor & the Opressed (25: 3–6, E121)

Paley thinks of this historical context as a third level of history in the poem:

> In 1806, Napoleon, who had crowned himself emperor two years earlier, amalgamated his conquered and allied German states into the Confederation of the Rhine. The Rhine valley, well known as a great wine-producing region, provides material for a powerful statement of Blake's apocalyptic vision. (2011: 802)

Against the backdrop of the end of times, the sons and daughters of Luvah tread the Wine-press. Mankind is described as Human grapes in the Wine-presses experiencing torment. Animals dance around the Wine-press of Luvah. Humanity is in a hell in which animals are the devils. The Wine-press is war in the spiritual world, war as it is seen in eternity. While its violence is suggestive of history itself, contemporary warfare in Europe, it is also an image of cultivation, and therefore of the other dimension of apocalypse: restoration. Foreshadowing the end of the poem, where history is spoken of as a Word, the printing press is brought into metaphorical identification with the war which is also cultivation:

> This Wine-Press is call'd War on Earth, it is the Printing-Press
> Of Los; and here he lays his words in order above the mortal brain
> As cogs are formd in a wheel to turn the cogs of the adverse wheel (27.8-10, E124)

When they speak, the sons of Luvah paradoxically declare that there will be no further cultivation until the last vintage is over, and, making the declaration more intriguing, they describe the last vintage not only in terms of harvest but the beginnings of cultivation, which makes us think of Rintrah and Palamabron again:

> ... This is the Last Vintage! & Seed
> Shall no more be sown upon Earth, till all the Vintage is over
> And all gatherd in, till the Plow has passd over the Nations

And the Harrow & heavy thundering Roller upon the mountains
(25.8-11, E121)

But then they change the focus in their speech. In Scripture, we read of how the Son of Man will separate nations from one another 'as a shepherd separates sheep from goats' (Matthew 25: 31–32). Interpreting the vision literally, the sons conclude that time has come and advocate a diabolic hierarchy, which reminds us of what Rintrah and Palamabron said of Swedenborg:

> ... Oh God deliver us to the Heavens or to the Earths,
> That we may preach righteousness & punish the sinner with death
> (25.13-14, E121)

Again Los speaks, offering verbal resistance. He addresses the sons of Luvah as 'Fellow Labourers', but his is a sociopolitical performative: he is clearly a *primus inter pares* endowed with the power to exhort and instruct. He endeavours to convey to his addressees a sense of where in sacred history they are and what they must do at this juncture. The reader is ready for much of what Los says, but a small number of comments may be useful. Los begins by confirming that the (last) vintage and harvest are reaching their conclusions and employing the image of the restoration of Albion. Golgonooza, closely associated with Albion, is approaching completion, owing to the accumulation of human endeavours in the arts, science, law and trade, the domains of human civilization. In preparation for the end, the sons must ignore the categories of family and nation, illusory groupings which are the product of Fall. Nations war with one another, but the real distinction is between the spiritual classes. The creeds of the different classes are repeated. When he speaks to Rintrah and Palamabron, he emphasizes that Milton must not be committed to the furnaces; now we learn about the fate that the Elect must face. The redeemed and reprobate may be prepared for the fires of Eternal Death ('consummation', fire and sexual union), but the Elect will take on the form of the Churches of Beulah. Los exhorts the sons to go on with their work ('Go forth Reapers with rejoicing'). He implores them to abstain from rest, continuing their labours just a little longer, so that they may 'Reap the whole Earth, from Pole to Pole', enjoying the ultimate harvest. Apocalypse will begin in Lambeth (in London). Blake closely associates Lambeth with Jerusalem in his poetry; here, Lambeth is identified as a woman, (like Jerusalem) and spoken of as 'Jerusalems inner court'. The emphasis

Opposition to Milton

is on its fallenness: the Blakes themselves lived in Lambeth for a time and returned to it after the sojourn in Felpham, and clearly there is a note of personal sadness owing to the condition of Lambeth. Los characterizes that fallenness through further allusions to the Hellenic, although here they are coupled with reference to Nordic mythology. Los reports how, addressing her as another female figure, Lambeth mourns over Jerusalem, but Jerusalem is also a city which will 'overspread all Nations'. He concludes his speech with a rapid sequence of commands: they must renounce the pleasures the weak succumb to, while treating the weak as their 'infant care'; they must not allow wrath to take hold of them; they must wait till the Last Judgement is past. Apocalypse is emblematized in the union of Christ (the Lamb) with his Church (his bride). The Supper of the Lamb lies on the other side of Judgement, and when the creation is consumed, the sons may rush forward with Los into 'glorious spiritual vegetation'. Los begins and ends his speech with references to the resurrection, the awakening of Albion, bound up with apocalypse:

> Fellow Labourers! The Great Vintage & Harvest is now upon Earth
> The whole extent of the Globe is explored: Every scatterd Atom
> Of Human Intellect now is flocking to the sound of the Trumpet
> All the Wisdom which was hidden in caves & dens, from ancient
> Time; is now sought out from Animal & Vegetable & Mineral
> The Awakener is come. outstretchd over Europe! the Vision of God is fulfilled
> The Ancient Man upon the Rock of Albion Awakes,
> He listens to the sounds of War astonishd & ashamed;
> He sees his Children mock at Faith and deny Providence
> Therefore you must bind the Sheaves not by Nations or Families
> You shall bind them in Three Classes; according to their Classes
> So shall you bind them. Separating What has been Mixed
> Since Men began to be Wove into Nations by Rahab & Tirzah
> Since Albions Death & Satans Cutting-off from our awful Fields;
> When under pretence to benevolence the Elect Subdud All
> From the Foundation of the World. The Elect is one Class: You
> Shall bind them separate: they cannot Believe in Eternal Life
> Except by Miracle & a New Birth. The other two Classes;
> The Reprobate who never cease to Believe, and the Redeemd,
> Who live in doubts & fears perpetually tormented by the Elect

> These you shall bind in a twin-bundle for the Consummation--
> But the Elect must be saved [from] fires of Eternal Death,
> To be formed into the Churches of Beulah that they destroy not the Earth
> For in every Nation & every Family the Three Classes are born
> And in every Species of Earth, Metal, Tree, Fish, Bird & Beast.
> We form the Mundane Egg, that Spectres coming by fury or amity
> All is the same, & every one remains in his own energy
> Go forth Reapers with rejoicing. you sowed in tears
> But the time of your refreshing cometh, only a little moment
> Still abstain from pleasure & rest, in the labours of eternity
> And you shall Reap the whole Earth, from Pole to Pole! from Sea to Sea
> Begining at Jerusalems Inner Court, Lambeth ruin'd and given
> To the detestable Gods of Priam, to Apollo: and at the Asylum
> Given to Hercules, who labour in Tirzahs Looms for bread
> Who set Pleasure against Duty: who Create Olympic crowns
> To make Learning a burden & the Work of the Holy Spirit: Strife.
> T[o] Thor & cruel Odin who first reard the Polar Caves
> Lambeth mourns calling Jerusalem. she weeps & looks abroad
> For the Lords coming, that Jerusalem may overspread all Nations
> Crave not for the mortal & perishing delights, but leave them
> To the weak, and pity the weak as your infant care; Break not
> Forth in your wrath lest you also are vegetated by Tirzah
> Wait till the Judgement is past, till the Creation is consumed
> And then rush forward with me into the glorious spiritual
> Vegetation; the Supper of the Lamb & his Bride; and the
> Awaking of Albion our friend and ancient companion. (25:17-62, E121-122)

Just as Rintrah and Palamabron remained unconvinced by his speech, so it seems Luvah's sons are similarly unmoved by Los's words (25.63-65, E122). But the sons offer no further resistance, Los's combative sociopolitical speech apparently having had something of the desired (perlocutionary) effect.

Note

1 Hilton suggests that the term 'Cathedron' is tied in with the fact that Blake's 'mother, sister and wife were all called Catherine' (1983: 113).

References

Blake, W. (1988), *The Complete Poetry and Prose of William Blake: Newly Revised Edition*, ed. D. V. Erdman, University of California Press: Berkeley.

Bloom, H. (1982), 'Commentary' in *The Complete Poetry and Prose of William Blake*, ed.D.V. Erdman, Berkeley: University of California Press, 894–972.

Damon, S.F. (1988), *A Blake Dictionary: The Ideas and Symbols of William Blake*, Hanover: University Press of New England.

Fox, S. (1976), *Poetic Form in Blake's Milton*, Princeton: Princeton University Press.

Frye, N. (2004), *Fearful Symmetry: A Study of William Blake*, ed.N. Halmi, Toronto: University of Toronto Press.

Frye, N. (2005), *Northrop Frye on Milton and Blake*, ed.A. Esterhammer, Toronto: University of Toronto Press.

Hilton, N. (1983), *Literal Imagination: Blake's Vision of Words*. Berkeley: University of California Press.

Howard, J. (1976), *Blake's Milton: A Study in Selfhood*, London: Associated University Presses.

Paley, M. (2011), 'William Blake's *Milton/A Poem* and the Miltonic Matrix of 1791–1810'. *University of Toronto Quarterly* 80.4 (2011): 786–814.

5 The Descent of Ololon

Before we learn about Los's joining with Milton-Blake and the journey of Blake, Milton and Los to Golgonooza (and immediately after the second account of Milton's uniting with Blake), we are told of a river of 'mild & liquid pearl/ Namd Ololon' (21.15–16, E115), who is many rather than one. Ololon are closely associated with figures dwelling on the banks of the river, who, we learn are the Eternals 'who Milton drove/ Down into Ulro' (21.16–17, E115). As we move forward, it is simply 'Ololon', an emanation figure, who are associated with driving Milton into Ulro. Howards states that

> Now Ololon is no longer identifiable as a group of eternals. Now Ololon has become a female, an emanation of Milton himself. This surprising shift of identity from eternals to emanation, however, can be explained if one recalls that earlier in the poem Milton's sixfold emanation is said to have a human (i.e., eternal) portion (17.3–4) just as Milton had. The fiery circle of wrathful eternals has always been Milton's emanations. Their sudden change here indicates that the split is about to be healed. (1976: 232)

On another level, of course, Milton has descended voluntarily because he is without his emanation; but Ololon are in the dark about these important details. Taking full responsibility for Milton's descent, Ololon weep 'in long resounding song/ For seven days of eternity' (21.17–18, E115). If, like the zoas, they initially viewed Milton as an antagonistic figure, by this stage, they have gained greater insight:

> ... for now they knew too late
> That it was Milton the Awakener: they had not heard the Bard,
> Whose song calld Milton to the attempt (21.32–34, E116)

DOI: 10.4324/9781003342571-6

92   *The Descent of Ololon*

Ololon then announce their decision to descend like Milton, although we should be careful about separating their descent from Milton's. As Fox observes, 'As Milton entered into his shadow, Ololon enters the "world beneath". The acts are identical; both are acts of repentance, both lead to eternal death, both herald apocalypse' (1976: 94). A small number of key declarations are central to this descent, which reaches a conclusion in both Golgonooza and Blake's garden in Felpham, and we might proceed by considering them. From the point of view of the present study, what is most striking is that Ololon's speech acts are never agonistic; as we shall see, they fall into other categories.

Eden

Ololon are first inspired to make a key declaration about descending. They deliver a short soliloquy, comprising an extended first-person plural imperative, effecting an exhortation about descending. A theme they will expand on, they begin to contrast the fallen world and Eternity. Asking themselves about the nature of the fallen world, Ololon toy with the idea that this world is a refuge, before turning to their own feelings, specifically repentance. Of great importance is the new insight about the nature of virtue: 'Is Virtue a Punisher'. The question, argues James, 'refers back to the Bard's analysis of the interdependence of vengeance and false virtue in Satan's moral codes and also indicates [Ololon's] precise role in Milton's regeneration' (1977: 113); but it is also a *mea culpa* with respect to the wrath which drove Milton as the Eighth Eye down into Ulro:

> ... Let us descend also, and let us give
> Ourselves to death in Ulro among the Transgressors.
> Is Virtue a Punisher? O no! how is this wondrous thing?
> This World beneath, unseen before: this refuge from the wars
> Of Great Eternity! unnatural refuge! unknown by us till now!
> Or are these the pangs of repentance? let us enter into them
> (21.45-50, E116)

The descent is the perlocutionary effect of the speech.

The Divine Family then verbally sanctions Ololon's proposed descent, their pronouncement itself also part of the manifold perlocutionary effect of Ololon's words. Deepening Ololon's understanding, they reveal to Ololon that it was not simply a matter of Ololon driving Milton out of heaven. Like Los, who knows that Milton is to have a crucial role in history, the Divine Family understand Milton's and

Ololon's descents in terms of a 'Universal Dictate' (21.53, E116). The Family issue a command: Ololon are to renew the world to 'Eternal Life' (21.57, E116). But Ololon are also given a warning – they (Ololon) will not be able to renew Milton. Ololon will not be able to follow the dictate of pity in that regard. Combining the command with this warning, the Divine Family makes the following performative pronouncement, clearly characterized by august sociopolitical authority:

> ... Six Thousand Years are now
> Accomplish'd in this World of Sorrow; Miltons Angel knew
> The Universal Dictate; and you also feel this Dictate.
> And now you know this World of Sorrow, and feel Pity. Obey
> The Dictate! Watch over this World, and with your brooding wings,
> Renew it to Eternal Life: Lo! I am with you alway
> But you cannot renew Milton he goes to Eternal Death (21.51–57, E116).

Earlier, the 'family/ Of Eden', having heard the laments, intervenes. They unite to form 'One Man' and approach Ololon:

> But all the Family Divine collected as Four Suns
> In the Four Points of heaven East, West & North & South
> Enlarging and enlarging till their Disks approachd each other;
> And when they touch'd closed together Southward in One Sun
> Over Ololon: and as One Man, who weeps over his brother,
> In a dark tomb, so all the Family Divine. wept over Ololon.
> (21.37–42, E116)

We are now told that when the Divine Family speak to Ololon of the Universal Dictate, they do so as Jesus, and, exploring the perlocutionary effect of that speech, Blake tells us of how Christ then appears in the clouds of Ololon:

> So spake the Family Divine as One Man even Jesus
> Uniting in One with Ololon & the appearance of One Man
> Jesus the Saviour appeard coming in the Clouds of Ololon!
> (21.58–60, E116)

Howard suggests that the dictate absorbed by Ololon refers back to necessity that 'one must die for another throughout all Eternity' (11.18, E105), and that their uniting is specifically the result of their understanding that necessity (1976: 233). James argues that 'following Milton, [they descend] to replace the "virtue" of punishment by the true virtue of forgiveness' (1977: 113). Of course the speech also segues to the account of Los's joining Blake (22.4–14, E116–117), and so, through juxtaposition, that development is also rendered an effect of Ololon's words.

Beulah

The end section of Book I is dedicated to describing Golgonooza: what Milton and Blake see and what we as readers learn of. At the start of Book II, we are provided with a kind of creation myth for Beulah, where Beulah is metaphorically a shadow, no doubt a shadow of Eden, brought into existence as a result of a speech act. Frye suggests that there is an important organic connection between the vision of Golgonooza at the end of Book I and this description:

> At the end of book 1, the whole objective world is seen as a creation of Los, and is thereby transformed into a responsive emanation, the Beulah described at the opening of book 2, from whence Ololon the milky way descends, like the angels descending Jacob's ladder (*M*, pl. 39, l. 35). (2005: 264)

Book II proceeds with 'all Ololon' descending from Eden into Beulah, weeping for Milton, and the Daughters of Beulah exhibiting a sense of wonder at the descent. The descent of Ololon into Beulah causes consternation. Howard usefully observes that 'The lamentations of Beulah are divided into four sections' (1976: 239). The next important speech occurs in the fourth section, and it is provided by Jesus. 'Since Jesus is present within Ololon', observes Summerfield, 'the Divine Voice can be heard within Beulah's songs of mourning, which in turn are contained in Ololon's lamentations' (1998: 257). Fox expertly explains who is being addressed and to what end:

> Beulah chants Jesus' castigation of Babylon, shadow of his emanation Jerusalem, whose vegetated jealousy has "Cut off my loves in fury till I have no love left for thee" (33:7). This is the prototypic male-female conflict, the cycle of jealousy and fear reflected in the relationships of Orc and the Shadowy Female and Milton and Ololon. But Jesus foresees an end to the cycle. Milton's descent will cause Ololon/Rahab to repent of her jealousy, and that in turn will bring Babylon to return Jerusalem to Jesus. (1976: 143)

As well as castigating Babylon, Jesus performatively enlightens her about the dynamics of the relations between male and female in eternity, about Ololon's destiny and about her (Babylon's) own future, which will undo the mischief generated by her jealousy:

> When I first Married you, I gave you all my whole Soul
> I thought that you would love my loves & joy in my delights
> Seeking for pleasures in my pleasures O Daughter of Babylon
> Then thou wast lovely, mild & gentle. now thou art terrible
> In jealousy & unlovely in my sight, because thou hast cruelly
> Cut off my loves in fury till I have no love left for thee
> Thy love depends on him thou lovest & on his dear loves
> Depend thy pleasures which thou hast cut off by jealousy
> Therefore I shew my jealousy & set before you Death
> Behold Milton descended to Redeem the Female Shade
> From Death Eternal; such your lot, to be continually Redeem'd
> By death & misery of those you love & by Annihilation
> When the Sixfold Female percieves that Milton annihilates
> Himself: that seeing all his loves by her cut off: he leaves
> Her also: intirely abstracting himself from Female loves
> She shall relent in fear of death: She shall begin to give
> Her maidens to her husband: delighting in his delight
> And then & then alone begins the happy Female joy
> As it is done in Beulah, & thou O Virgin Babylon Mother of Whoredoms
> Shalt bring Jerusalem in thine arms in the night watches; and
> No longer turning her a wandering Harlot in the streets
> Shalt give her into the arms of God your Lord & Husband
> (33.2–23, E132–133)

James argues that Ololon can hear this pronouncement, meaning that part of its perlocutionary impact involves how it serves to enlighten Ololon. He states, 'This reveals to Ololon the correct female role of free generosity and lack of possessiveness, antithetical to the perverse sexuality of the fallen state' (1977: 114).

Another pronouncement follows hot on the heels of the last. The Songs of the Daughters of Beulah register surprise that the aggression of Ololon has been changed to concern and pity for Milton. There is a performative element here, too: by speaking, the Daughters evolve their own understanding, and, in another regard, the illocutionary effect is the proffering of consolation, despite the role Ololon played in Milton's descent into Ulro:

Are you the Fiery Circle that late drove in fury & fire
The Eight Immortal Starry-Ones down into Ulro dark
Rending the Heavens of Beulah with your thunders & lightnings
And can you thus lament & can you pity & forgive?
Is terror changd to pity O wonder of Eternity! (34.3–7, E133)

Ulro

Ololon then proceed with their descent, leaving Beulah behind. They seek 'the Or Ulro & its fiery Gates' (34.19, E13), which is presented as the last of four States, which Frye suggests we think of as the emanations of the worlds which structure the action: here 'Beulah' is the emanation of Eden, Alla the emanation of Beulah, and Or-Ulro the emanation of Ulro, Al-Ulro being the emanation of our world of 'Generation' (Frye, 2005: 264). Fox suggests the Or-Ulro is Ulro seen 'through feminine eyes' (1976: 146).

From Milton's track, Ololon see Ulro and the Polypus. It stretches down to the fallen world; it is a twenty-seven-fold monstrosity; Rahab and her daughters (again) can be seen in it; they sing seductive songs in order to lure 'Sleepers of Beulah' down into the Dead Sea; but Los can also be seen building the Mundane Shell. The female figures in the Polypus are 'the sixfold emanation that is Ololon's own selfhood' (Howard, 1976: 242), who were pictured as the rocks of Horeb in the region of Midian (plate 17), but, as James argues, 'Ololon's self-conscious vision of these monstrous forms of Death, implying [Ololon's] separation from them, is an indication of [Ololon's] progressing freedom from the restrictive ossification Milton's earthly female family imposed on him' (1977: 114).

The focus shifts to the 'Four Universes round the Universe of Los' (visualized in the design of plate 32) and then to the sons of Ololon, before we hear of how Ololon respond as they (Ololon) look down 'into the heavens of Ulro' (34.49, E134). Ololon produce another soliloquy, although this time their speech is constative. They are struck by the stark contrast between how things are in eternity and how they are in Ulro. The 'wars of man in Great Eternity' appears in a parodic form in Ulro, which means that they are connected to physical death. In their Ulro manifestations, flora and fauna as well as 'Visions of Human Life & Shadows of Widsom & Knowledge' (34.55, E135) appear frozen compared to their realities in eternity. The plants and animals are also subject to death and decay, while the fauna 'Are here frozen to unexpansive deadly destroying terrors' (35.1, E135). In Eternity, War and Hunting are intellectual and creative endeavours; in Ulro the two

The Descent of Ololon 97

activities which go by those names are parodies of eternal activities. In Eternity, fraternity is also intellectual; in Ulro 'Brotherhood is changed into a Curse & a Flattery' (35.4, E135). Then we return to the vision of Rahab, Tirzah and her sisters as well as the Loom of Death. We know that 'Cathedrons Looms weave only Death' (24.35, E120), but the role is attributed exclusively to the six figures in this instance: they weave the 'Woof of Death' (35.8, E135) across a London 'Where once the Cherubs of Jerusalem spread to Lambeth's Vale' (35.10, E135):

How are the Wars of Man which in Great Eternity
Appear around, in the External Spheres of Visionary Life
Here renderd Deadly within the Life & Interior Vision
How are the Beasts & Birds & Fishes, & Plants & Minerals
Here fixd into a frozen bulk subject to decay & death
Those Visions of Human Life & Shadows of Wisdom & Knowledge
Are here frozen to unexpansive deadly destroying terrors
And War & Hunting: the Two Fountains of the River of Life
Are become Fountains of bitter Death & of corroding Hell
Till Brotherhood is changd into a Curse & a Flattery
By Differences between Ideas, that Ideas themselves, (which are
The Divine Members) may be slain in offerings for sin
O dreadful Loom of Death! O piteous Female forms compelld
To weave the Woof of Death, On Camberwell Tirzahs Courts
Malahs on Blackheath, Rahab & Noah. dwell on Windsors heights
Where once the Cherubs of Jerusalem spread to Lambeths Vale
Milcahs Pillars shine from Harrow to Hampstead where Hoglah
On Highgates heights magnificent Weaves over trembling Thames
To Shooters Hill and thence to Blackheath the dark Woof! Loud
Loud roll the Weights & Spindles over the whole Earth let down
On all sides round to the Four Quarters of the World, eastward on
Europe to Euphrates & Hindu, to Nile & back in Clouds
Of Death across the Atlantic to America North & South
(34.50–35.17, E134–135)

Ololon examine the 'Couches of the Dead' (35.26, E135): Los's, Enitharmon's, and those of the Sons of Albion and the zoas. They see Milton's couch, too; at this point they see the 'Eight/Immortal Starry-Ones' (35.29-30, E135), whereupon we are presented (for a second time) with Ololon expressing their regret at having actuated Milton. Although the speech is merely reported, it is a crucial development.

Ololon, having seen the Starry Eight guarding Milton's death couch, ask them for forgiveness and confess their crime. Again, Fox expertly highlights the simultaneity of the action:

> Ololon's falling down prostrate is the moral analogue of her descent. It is the act of contrition we saw briefly in Book I, seen now from the perspective of the polypus and not through the clarified fourfold vision of Blake/Milton. The change in perspective seems to be a change in the *dramatis personae*: in Book I Ololon confessed to the Divine Family, who, uniting with her, became Jesus. Here she begs forgiveness of the Starry Eight, of the Seven Angels of the Presence and the eighth, apocalyptic angel who is Milton himself, no longer dark but restored to brilliance by union with Ololon. (1976: 150)

The Starry Eight are overjoyed by the descent of Ololon. As though looking over Ololon's shoulder, they see 'a wide road' (35.35, E135) from Ulro back to Eternity; they also see 'the Lord in the Clouds of Ololon' (35.41, E136), an association already established, which foreshadows the conclusion of the vision.

Golgonooza II: Context V

We are then told of how Ololon enter Golgonooza. Two further speech acts are important to Ololon's descent, but before considering them we should turn to what we learn about Golgonooza in this section of the poem.

Prior to Ololon's prostrating themselves before the Starry Eight and asking forgiveness, it is clarified that no one can behold Golgonooza before they pass the Polypus, and that only Christ can pass through the Polypus without succumbing to annihilation. (It is only at this point that it becomes explicit that Golgonooza is Ololon's destination.) But having passed through the Polypus, one beholds Golgonooza, either as a fourfold vision, or a threefold vision, where, having become 'Mortal & Vegetable in Sexuality/[...] you behold its mighty Spires & Domes of ivory & gold' (35.24–25, E135). As Fox states, 'Mortal Blake passed inward to where he viewed and described Los's world "on all sides round"; immortal Ololon must, like Milton, pass the satanic polypus before she can join Blake there' (1976: 149).

After providing an account of the joy of the Starry Eight, Blake proceeds with his account of Ololon's journey, relating it through a striking double vision. Towards the end of Book I, Blake speaks of constellations, before turning to flies, and trees on mountains. He then tells us that these are manifestations of the Children of Los. Similarly, he speaks of natural phenomena as lamentations of Beulah. On plates 35 and 36, Blake begins to evolve another twofold vision, involving Golgonooza and other aspects of the invisible order of reality. The vision involves a small number of important natural symbols: a rock (the rock of Odours), a fountain, 'Wild Thyme' and the Lark, which ultimately may represent phenomena Blake experiences in the environs of his garden in Felpham, which is where the vision leads us. The continuation of Ololon's progress will be told mostly in terms of how that progress appears from a temporal point of view – from the temporal side of the double vision.

We learned earlier about the 'Moment in each Day that Satan cannot find' (35.42, E136); Ololon use this moment: 'In this Moment Ololon descended to Los & Enitharmon/ Unseen beyond the Mundane Shell Southward in Miltons track' (35.46–47, E136). Invoking the Wild Thyme and the fountain, the moment gets associated with 'a Fountain in a rock' (35.49, E136). Blake tells us of how it divides into two streams, and as he provides us with an account of their paths, a double vision reveals how these features of the natural world are actually bound up with Golgonooza and Blake's other levels of reality:

> Just in this Moment when the morning odours rise abroad
> And first from the Wild Thyme, stands a Fountain in a rock
> Of crystal flowing into two Streams, one flows thro Golgonooza
> And thro Beulah to Eden beneath Los's western Wall
> The other flows thro the Aerial Void & all the Churches
> Meeting again in Golgonooza beyond Satans Seat (35.48–53, E136)

Fox again does justice to the simultaneity of the action:

> In this moment Ololon's lamentation was heard in eternity, and "Providence began" (21:24); "In this Moment Ololon descended to Los & Enitharmon". Lamentation and descent, we see once again, are identical' (1976: 152).

Expanding the vision, the Wild Thyme is then identified as 'Los's Messenger to Eden':

> The Wild Thyme is Los's Messenger to Eden, a mighty Demon
> Terrible deadly & poisonous his presence in Ulro dark

Therefore he appears only a small Root creeping in grass
Covering over the Rock of Odours his bright purple mantle
Beside the Fount above the Larks nest in Golgonooza (35.54-58, E136)

The focus then shifts to the all-important figure of the lark, which in the double vision is 'a mighty Angel' (36.12, E136). Blake describes a process involving crystal gates and a total of twenty-eight larks, beginning with the twenty-seventh. Each gate is an entrance to one of the Heavens of Beulah. We are told of how the first lark rises towards a gate which is an entrance to 'the First Heaven named Luther' (35.62, E136). (Luther, we remember is the twenty-seventh church.) This is the beginning of a process which stretches back to the last heaven (the first church, Adam) and beyond. In Blake's imagery, the Seven Eyes of God walk through the twenty-seven Churches towards Satan's seat. The larks have the job of preventing the Eyes from falling into 'slumber nor sleep' (35.65, E136). On reaching 'the highest lift of his light pinions' (36.1, E136), the first lark encounters the second lark '& back to back/ They touch their pinions tip: and each descend/ To their respective Earths' (36.2-4, E136). They carry news upon their wings, and 'consult with Angels/ Of Providence & with the Eyes of God all night in slumbers/ Inspired' (364-6, E136). Clearly, it is of great significance that, while there are twenty-seven heavens, this process involves twenty-eight larks. Without the twenty-eighth, the sequence would be suggestive of circle, beginning in this account with Luther and ending with Adam, before beginning all over again. But the twenty-eighth is suggestive of transcendence; perhaps the larks now move through what now may be thought of as a spiral rather than a cycle.

Felpham/Golgonooza

Ololon's story is told in connection with this process and with the double vision in question. We are first told that she 'sat beside this Fountain on the Rock of Odours' (35.60, E136). Then the two worlds of the double vision are brought together in such a way as to bring Ololon into Blake's garden even if she (we can certainly say 'she' at this point) is still in Golgonooza.

> ... the Twenty-eighth bright
> Lark. met the Female Ololon descending into my Garden
> Thus it appears to Mortal eyes & those of the Ulro Heavens
> But not thus to Immortals (36.9-12, E136)

The Descent of Ololon · 101

As Fox suggests, 'The garden in which Ololon appears is the tangible portion of Golgonooza; it is where Blake's mortal part was carried when his imagination entered the city of art' (1976: 154). Ololon, we are informed, stepped into the Polypus. When they stepped into the Polypus, they become singular, 'One Female' (36.16, E137). She is now a virgin, but, as such, an inimical figure, like the Lady of Milton's *Comus* as Blake reads Milton's masque (Frye, 2004: 344–345). In this form, she suddenly appears in Blake's garden.

When Los and Blake become one, which, from the narrator's point of view, is three years ago at this stage, Los provides Blake with a cottage where he can write – we might think of *Milton* as an unfinished poem at the *fabula* stage we have reached. Felpham is to Golgonooza what Lambeth is to Ulro. Blake has knowledge of Golgonooza by this stage. But the vision which ensues will ultimately represent a counterpart to the vision of Golgonooza.

Blake's task is to 'display Nature's cruel holiness' (36.25, E137), and the Ololon who stands before him may be a symbol of that holiness. But he is apparently oblivious to this. He addresses her courteously as a Daughter of Beulah, and therefore as a source of inspiration. Blake understands she is a messenger and clarifies that he is ready to respond to her prompts, even if it means persisting with his labours which bring him and his wife misery. He also asks if she might take care of Catherine, who is poorly: we know Catherine was suffering from ague and rheumatism at this point (Apesos, 2015: 386). Blake's performative comes nowhere close to having the expected perlocutionary effect. Ololon ignores it and declares, in a non-combative statement that will prove to have a manifold perlocutionary effect (as we shall see in the next chapter), that her business is with Milton:

And as One Female, Ololon and all its mighty Hosts
Appear'd: a Virgin of twelve years nor time nor space was
To the perception of the Virgin Ololon but as the
Flash of lightning but more quick the Virgin in my Garden
Before my Cottage stood for the Satanic Space is delusion…

Walking in my Cottage Garden, sudden I beheld
The Virgin Ololon & address'd her as a Daughter of Beulah[:]

Virgin of Providence fear not to enter into my Cottage
What is thy message to thy friend: What am I now to do
Is it again to plunge into deeper affliction? behold me
Ready to obey, but pity thou my Shadow of Delight
Enter my Cottage, comfort her, for she is sick with fatigue
The Virgin answer'd. Knowest thou of Milton who descended

Driven from Eternity; him I seek! terrified at my Act
In Great Eternity which thou knowest! I come him to seek (36:16-36:20, 36:26-37:3, E136-137)

References

Apesos, A. (2015), 'The Poet in the Poem: Blake's *Milton*'. *Studies in Philology* 112.2: 379–413.

Blake, W. (1988), *The Complete Poetry and Prose of William Blake: Newly Revised Edition*, ed. D. V. Erdman, University of California Press: Berkeley.

Fox, S. (1976), *Poetic Form in Blake's Milton*, Princeton: Princeton University Press.

Frye, N. (2004), *Fearful Symmetry: A Study of William Blake*, ed.N. Halmi, Toronto: University of Toronto Press.

Frye, N. (2005), *Northrop Frye on Milton and Blake*, ed.A. Esterhammer, Toronto: University of Toronto Press.

Howard, J. (1976), *Blake's Milton: A Study in Selfhood*, London: Associated University Presses.

James, D. (1977), *Written Within and Without: A Study of Blake's Milton*, Frankfurt: Peter Lang.

Summerfield, H. (1998), *A Guide to the Books of William Blake for Innocent and Experienced Readers*, Gerards Cross: Colin Smythe.

6 The Redemption of the Contraries

Blake works with different schemata in his poem. The best way to approach the end of the poem is in terms of its being a continuation of the very beginning of the poem in terms of schema. The focus shifts back very clearly to Miltonic male and female principles. There is of course a doubleness to the principles. Satan figures in the conclusion, and, again, he represents Milton's 'double' or spectre. In addition, the female principle proves to be twofold.

Milton and Satan

As Frye observes, 'The emanation retreats from anyone who seeks her in the outside world, but appears when the natural perspective is reversed; hence the paradox that although the object of Milton's journey is to seek Ololon, Ololon in fact seeks him' (2005a: 264). The illocutionary force of Ololon's words is enough to produce a reaction. In the form of a combination of Shadow and human form, Milton descends, his descent the perlocutionary effect of Ololon's words, even if it is also his Bard's Song which inspires the descent.

The Shadow (Blake sees) also contains the 'Monstrous Churches of Beulah, the Gods of Ulro dark' (37.16, E137). The three groups of churches are alluded to and their sexual identities are spoken of. What gets introduced for the first time in the poem at this point are names of the churches, nine which are 'Giant mighty Hermaphroditic' and eleven which are 'Female-Males', along with which seven are 'Male-Females' (37.35–43, E138).

The gods are demonic figures drawn from the account of the fallen angels of Milton's *Paradise Lost* (i:391–513). They are Baal, Ashtaroth, Chemosh, Molech, Dagon, Thammuz, Rimmon, Belial, Saturn, Jove and Rhea, plus a character complex comprising Osiris, Isis and Orus (Horus). A number of important associations surround these figures.

DOI: 10.4324/9781003342571-7

104 *The Redemption of the Contraries*

Blake speaks of 'Chaotic Voids outside of the Stars [which] are measured by/ The Stars, which are the boundaries of Kingdoms, Provinces/ And Empires of Chaos' (37.47–49, E138). He thinks of each of the gods as fourfold, and he associates them with these stellar dominions, specifically the forty-eight districts of the kingdoms of two giants, Og and Sihon, belonging to the grouping we came across earlier. These districts, in turn, are identified as the 'Forty-eight Starry Regions' (38.1, E138) of the combination of Orion (the southern constellations and the zodiac) and Ophiucus (the twenty-one northern constellations). And it emerges that this star-world is identifiable with the Mundane Shell:

> From Star to Star, Mountains & Valleys, terrible dimension
> Stretchd out, compose the Mundane Shell, a mighty Incrustation
> Of Forty-eight deformed Human Wonders of the Almighty
> With Caverns whose remotest bottoms meet again beyond
> The Mundane Shell in Golgonooza. (37.52–56, E138)

The churches or heavens and the gods are explicitly identified with the Cherub (something already suggested by Rintrah and Palamabron) and Satan, respectively: 'The Heavens are the Cherub, the Twelve Gods are Satan' (37.60, E138). The regions also get identified with the 'Cities of the Levites' (38.1, E138) and the Polypus.

The perlocutionary effect is not complete, however. Milton now emerges from his Shadow, appearing in Blake's garden 'clothed in black, severe & silent' (38.8, E138). Fox argues that Milton's attire is identifiable with the 'robe of the promise' he removed after hearing the Bard's Song. Hence, the focus is still that moment. Milton's appearance, then, 'is simultaneous with his original decision, but yet it is a kind of slow-motion close-up of that act, which was completed in Book I but will not be complete in Book II until the dark garments of the promise are annihilated' (1976: 161).

No sooner have we learned about Milton's arrival in Felpham than it is revealed that Satan has also appeared as a separate entity off the coast (apparently, on the water) not far from Blake's Felpham cottage – it seems this is also eventuated by what has been happening, and partly by Ololon's speech. Communicating through thunder, Satan has an aggressive bearing towards Milton, but for all his bluster he is unable to harm him:

> The Spectre of Satan stood upon the roaring sea & beheld
> Milton within his sleeping Humanity! trembling & shuddring
> He stood upon the waves a Twenty-seven-fold mighty Demon

Gorgeous & beautiful: loud roll his thunders against Milton
Loud Satan thunderd, loud & dark upon mild Felpham shore
Not daring to touch one fibre he howld round upon the Sea.
(38.9–14, E139)

On account of both Satan's being an attribute of Milton and the union of the two poets, Blake may also describe Satan's bosom *from within*. It is described almost entirely in terms of mineral imagery. It has recognizable architectural features, but also ruins like the ones Shelley's traveller speaks of in 'Ozymandias'; its mineral imagery includes ore, pitch and nitre – emphasis is also placed on 'plains of burning sand' (38.17, E139).

Milton's Triumph over Satan

The stunning conclusion of the poem begins at this point. Strikingly, the various dimensions of the poem are simultaneously present. In addition to what is happening in Felpham, Milton's redeemed is still fighting with Urizen on the banks of the Arnon. So, the reality is that Milton is in a struggle with Urizen's unfallen and fallen dimensions in distinct domains. Slightly later, Blake will helpfully clarify the nature of the relationship between this manifestation of Milton and the redeemed Milton we followed in Chapter 3: that redeemed self or spirit is like the 'Thought' of the figure who now emerges from the Shadow. Blake comments:

> ... as the Plowman or Artificer or Shepherd
> While in the labours of his Calling sends his Thought abroad
> To labour in the ocean or in the starry heaven. So Milton
> Labourd in Chasms of the Mundane Shell, tho here before
> My Cottage. (39.54–58, E141)

The episode in which Los joins Blake is also present in the sense that, from the temporal viewpoint, that episode is part of the biography of the Blake we come across now. We have no way of knowing how much Blake has gained as a result of the union or even how conscious of the moment of union he is at this point. The Blake who narrates – the homodiegetic Blake – knows of the union and its full significance; the intradiegetic Blake – the Blake in the narrative – may not yet know of the union, but it has occurred, and we know that he has been hard at work on 'these Visions' (36.24, E137), which are the result of the union. Additionally, it may seem as though what happens over the protracted ending of Book II 'happens to' Milton, but the very end of the poem establishes (again) the fact that it is also happening to Blake: the experience is also *his* visionary experience. As we have seen, Catherine Blake will find Blake splayed on their garden path, after he has collapsed under the intensity of the vision.

I said in Chapter 2 that such is the significance of Milton's personality that, because he failed to achieve full self-development, sacred history and therefore human history *continued*. It follows on from this that full self-development will not be confined to Milton and his emanation. If he can complete the development of self, history will proceed to a kind of conclusion or consummation.

It is of course speech which eventuates the all-important developments. The speech is performative; more particularly, it is unequivocally phenomenological. By producing self-transforming language, Milton *secures* the instant before apocalypse.

First of all, Milton makes a great speech, addressed to Satan, the speech effecting his victory over his own Spectre. Before turning to this speech, we might profitably turn to an earlier one. Earlier in Book II, within the context of the lamentation of Beulah over Ololon, Milton's 'real and immortal self' takes lessons from the Seven Angels of the Presence. The illocutionary force of their words serves to enlighten Milton. They begin by establishing they are States comprising individuals – we should think of them as multitudes. They possess 'Human Form', bestowed by 'Divine Humanity & Mercy', and they contrast themselves with those whom Satan 'combind' into 'Shapeless Rocks', exhibiting 'Satans Mathematic Holiness'. The latter represent 'a corrupted form of the Seven Eyes forced into becoming the selfhood's tools for destructive moralism, and restrictive control [as well as] mathematical delusion' (Howard, 1976: 96). The former 'have maintained a free and brotherly relationship, so that their forms, though imperfect, contrast with the forms of those who have succumbed to Satan's love of war and his belief that reality can be mathematically defined' (Summerfield, 1998, 255). A biographical detail creeps in, because those subject to 'Satans Tyranny' calumniate 'Human Imagination'. The Angels explain to Milton that the crucial distinction is between States and Individuals. Strikingly, Individuals are not subject to change; states do change, however. States change in that the Seven are a sequence which unfolds over time. Returning to the theme of 'Eternal Death', they observe that it is impossible to proceed to 'Eternal Death in that which can never die'. There is no Eternal Death as an individual. Satan and Adam are referenced as States, but it is only through a new State, 'Eternal Annihilation', identifiable with Milton, that it is possible to proceed to Eternal Death.

The Redemption of the Contraries 107

Milton is to go to 'Eternal Death', but only part of the self may proceed to that death: the eternal self avoids Eternal Death. The 'Imagination', identified with 'Human Existence itself', endures. So too does Love if conjoined to the Imagination. But Love divided from Imagination, memory and Reason may all proceed to annihilation. As James argues, Milton 'needs to separate out his real and eternal self from the various corrupt temporary forms of self existing in time and space' (1977: 86). The Angels add that States are created, and that it is created things which can be annihilated. They complete their disquisition by turning to 'Forms', which exist eternally. Such forms might make us think of Platonic forms, but, as Frye says, Eden 'is a world of forms like Plato's except that in Blake these forms are images of pure being seen by a spiritual body, not ideas of pure essence seen by a soul, a conception which would rule out the artist as a revealer of reality' (2005a: 296):

> We are not Individuals but States: Combinations of Individuals
> We Were Angels of the Divine Presence: & were Druids in Annandale
> Compelld to combine into Form by Satan, the Spectre of Albion,
> Who made himself a God &, destroyed the Human For Divine.
> But the Divine Humanity & Mercy gave us a Human Form
> Because we were combind in Freedom & holy Brotherhood
> While those combind by Satans Tyranny first in the blood of War
> And Sacrifice &, next, in Chains of imprisonment: are Shapeless Rocks
> Retaining only Satans Mathematic Holiness, Length: Bredth & Highth
> Calling the Human Imagination: which is the Divine Vision & Fruition
> In which Man liveth eternally: madness & blasphemy, against
> Its own Qualities, which are Servants of Humanity, not Gods or Lords
> Distinguish therefore States from Individuals in those States.
> States Change: but Individual Identities never change nor cease:
> You cannot go to Eternal Death in that which can never Die.
> Satan & Adam are States Created into Twenty-seven Churches
> And thou O Milton art a State about to be Created
> Called Eternal Annihilation that none but the Living shall
> Dare to enter: & they shall enter triumphant over Death
> And Hell & the Grave! States that are not, but ah! Seem to be.
>
> Judge then of thy Own Self: thy Eternal Lineaments explore
> What is Eternal & what Changeable? & what Annihilable!

108 *The Redemption of the Contraries*

> The Imagination is not a State: it is the Human Existence itself
> Affection or Love becomes a State, when divided from Imagination
> The Memory is a State always, & the Reason is a State
> Created to be Annihilated & a new Ratio Created
> Whatever can be Created can be Annihilated Forms cannot
> The Oak is cut down by the Ax, the Lamb falls by the Knife
> But their Forms Eternal Exist, For-ever. Amen Halle[l]ujah.
> (32.10-32.38, E131-132)

The perlocutionary effect of the Angels' speech becomes clear when Milton addresses Satan, confronting him with formidable resolve. Milton now knows Satan's *modus operandi*. He has understood that Satan's strength lies in his ability to make people believe in nothing other than the 'here and now', fearing illusory death so much that they will do anything, even malevolent acts, to extend their natural lives. The Bard's Song relates how the Elect are not to be destroyed; such a response merely produces a new tyranny. Hence, Milton's attitude to Satan counts as a perlocutionary effect of the Bard's Song, too. By giving in to Satan, one accepts one's role in a cyclical process whereby in defeating a tyrant through force one becomes tyrannical oneself – metaphorically, a 'covering' for the defeated tyrant, whose will one continues to execute, even if it appears one has overthrown a menace. His is now a creed of self-sacrifice, the creed of Christ and all reprobates. Milton now knows that what is lost when one rejects Satan's diabolic logic amounts to little compared with what one saves. What he is expressing is the exact opposite of a death-wish. Indeed, his speech represents the defeat of the opposite wish: the wish which consists in hanging on to one's natural life at any price. He speaks of preserving only that which is 'of God alone', and we know that this is the Imagination, the real self, that which is 'of God'. Milton is now the State called Eternal Annihilation. In a combative performative statement, he takes a giant leap towards defeating Satan and precipitating apocalypse:

> Satan! my Spectre! I know my power thee to annihilate
> And be a greater in thy place, & be thy Tabernacle
> A covering for thee to do thy will, till one greater comes
> And smites me as I smote thee & becomes my covering.
> Such are the Laws of thy false Heavns! but Laws of Eternity
> Are not such: know thou: I come to Self Annihilation
> Such are the Laws of Eternity that each shall mutually

The Redemption of the Contraries 109

Annihilate himself for others good, as I for thee[.]
Thy purpose & the purpose of thy Priests & of thy Churches
Is to impress on men the fear of death; to teach
Trembling & fear, terror, constriction; abject selfishness
Mine is to teach Men to despise death & to go on
In fearless majesty annihilating Self, laughing to scorn
Thy Laws & terrors, shaking down thy Synagogues as webs
I come to discover before Heavn & Hell the Self righteousness
In all its Hypocritic turpitude, opening to every eye
These wonders of Satans holiness shewing to the Earth
The Idol Virtues of the Natural Heart, & Satans Seat
Explore in all its Selfish Natural Virtue & put off
In Self annihilation all that is not of God alone:
To put off Self & all I have ever & ever Amen. (38.29–49, E139)

The perlocutionary effects of Milton's speech follow hot on the heels of the locution. First, it produces a defiant speech from Satan. Through language Satan tries to create a *persona* which Milton will take to be real. The self he wants to promote is organized around the royal metaphor. He speaks off all things as parts of his body, 'One Great Satan'. Of course the same kind of metaphor occurs in an apocalyptic context, where Christ is the royal metaphor, but here the context is diabolic parody. Satan may advance the argument that Christ is a 'Divine Delusion' (39.2, E140), but the opposite is true. Just as his 'Seven Angels' merely imitate the Eyes of God in a different context, so Satan as a single body is a parody of Christ. We might go so far as to call Satan's attitude 'totalitarian', which Frye calls 'the effort to conceive the state as a single body incarnate in its leader' (2006: 115). His speech begins with a performative, the aim of which is to secure submission, obedience and worship:

I am God the judge of all, the living & the dead
Fall therefore down & worship me. submit thy supreme
Dictate, to my eternal Will & to my dictate bow
I hold the Balances of Right & Just & mine the Sword
Seven Angels bear my Name & in those Seven I appear
But I alone am God & I alone in Heavn & Earth
Of all that live dare utter this, others tremble & bow
Till All Things become One Great Satan, in Holiness
Oppos'd to Mercy, and the Divine Delusion Jesus be no more.
(38.51–59, E139-140)

His is a powerful use of performative language; but his ability to do things with words appears diminished. Satan is faking the sociopolitical. Indeed, a perlocutionary effect, unfavourable to Satan, then impacts on the situation: rather than the corrupted Seven, the 'Starry Seven' appear. As Fox observes, 'the "Delusion" appears in the garden, and Satan is again caught defending a lie' (1976: 164). They manifest 'around Milton' on Blake's garden path. Addressing Albion, they exhort him to cast Satan into the fiery lake associated with Los. Satan is again referred to as the Spectre of Albion:

> Awake Albion awake! reclaim thy Reasoning Spectre. Subdue
> Him to the Divine Mercy, Cast him down into the Lake
> Of Los, that ever burneth with fire, ever & ever Amen!
> Let the Four Zoa's awake from Slumbers of Six Thousand Years.
> (39.10-13, E140)

Their speech does not immediately have the desired effect on Albion, but it has a decisive effect on Satan: again, a perlocutionary effect is crucial. It is at this point that we see that speech begins to change reality at the end of time in comparable way to how it had the same effect at the time of the Fall. Trembling (presumably with fear) and feeling astonishment, Satan morphs, revealing himself in the form of the evil quaternary, a demonic parody of the four zoas, consisting of Chaos, Sin, Death and Ancient Night. But his taking on this form points to his defeat: his strength lies in dissimulation. Howard convincingly suggests that a fourfold process of satanic revelation (each stage of which we have considered in this chapter) reaches a conclusion at this point. First, we have the 'revelation of the historic selfhood' (1976: 249); second, the revelation of 'the selfhood's hypocritic nature' (1976: 250); third, the false Satan's claiming that the starry seven belong to him (ibid.); and fourth, this moment in which he apes the divine humanity (1976: 251). His various ruses failing, he fails. In his response to the Bard's Song, Milton speaks of loosing Satan from his hells. If Matthews is right, and Milton looses Satan by ridding himself of his own satanic aspect (1980: 77), then Satan has now been 'freed'.

The focus returns to Albion trying to rise: from this point of view, it seems as though this time it is the words of the Starry Seven that actuate the giant form. His body is associated with British locations, and he 'turns throughout all England, his fallen body' (Fox, 1976: 166); but he falls back into his slumber, the time of his awakening still not having come.

Also a perlocutionary effect is a development in the conflict between Milton's redeemed self and Urizen. We said earlier that the battle between Milton and Urizen-Satan is being fought on two fronts, as it were. We now learn of a decisive victory on the other plane, precipitated by Milton's confronting Satan on this one:

> Urizen faints in terror striving among the Brooks of Arnon
> With Miltons Spirit. (39.53–54, E141)

The Contraries

We hear nothing more of Satan in the poem, although Milton has more to say about how to consolidate his own emerging victory. Next, we learn more of the perlocutionary effect of Milton's earlier words, the focus shifting back to Ololon, who speaks next. Ololon is able to see Milton's redeemed self's struggle with Urizen and the other zoas, although she makes no explicit reference to the victory of Milton's redeemed self. Her main focus is deism. She speaks of the paradox of a (in her view symbolically feminine) disposition which attacks religion, but only establishes another religion – a more absurd one – in its place. She alludes to a rogues' gallery of deists: this time, three eighteenth-century British public intellectuals are spoken of in the same breath as Voltaire and Rousseau in addition to Newton. In the second chapter, we gave consideration to how a particular kind of female figure representing the natural world is also suggestive of natural religion. We have seen how Rahab and Tirzah represent part of the female will, and how they are responsible for the appearance of Voltaire and Rousseau and therefore eighteenth-century natural religion. Ololon comprises Rahab and her daughters. She is more than this, but she has been unaware of that until now. Highlighting her connection with Rahab and her daughters, Ololon concludes that she, Milton's Emanation, is responsible for natural religion. The communication is unambiguously noncombative, but it will prove 'progressive' nonetheless. The exchange, as we shall see, permits her to progress to an understanding and a decision which will have far-reaching consequences. She declares,

> I see thee strive upon the Brooks of Arnon. there a dread
> And awful Man I see, oercoverd with the mantle of years.
> I behold Los & Urizen. I behold Orc & Tharmas;
> The Four Zoas of Albion & thy Spirit with them striving
> In Self annihilation giving thy life to thy enemies
> Are those who contemn Religion & seek to annihilate it

112   *The Redemption of the Contraries*

> Become in their Femin[in]e portions the causes & promoters
> Of these Religions, how is this thing? this Newtonian Phantasm
> This Voltaire & Rousseau: this Hume & Gibbon & Bolingbroke
> This Natural Religion! this impossible absurdity
> Is Ololon the cause of this? O where shall I hide my face
> These tears fall for the little-ones: the Children of Jerusalem
> Lest they be annihilated in thy annihilation. (40.4–16, E141)

Her speech proves an instance of the phenomenological performative. Her words clearly precipitate another reality-altering effect: the sudden appearance of 'Rahab Babylon', the real cause of natural religion. The perlocutionary effect of Ololon's words, Rahab appears 'Eastward upon the Paved work across Europe & Asia' (40.18, E141). Rahab is identified in the way we are familiar with now: 'A Female Hidden in a Male, Religion hidden in War' (40.20, E141). At this stage, Rahab, even though she also has some kind of objective existence, is still a part of Ololon. But even the inception of a sense that Rahab is something separable from Ololon proves sufficient to evoke this objective projection. The effect of Ololon's speech registers the moment she completes her speech act:

> No sooner she had spoke but Rahab Babylon appeard
> Eastward upon the Paved work across Europe & Asia
> Glorious as the midday Sun in Satans bosom glowing:
> A Female hidden in a Male, Religion hidden in War
> Namd Moral Virtue; cruel two-fold Monster shining bright
> A Dragon red & hidden Harlot which John in Patmos saw
>
> And all beneath the Nations innumerable of Ulro
> Appeard, the Seven Kingdoms of Canaan & Five Baalim
> Of Philistea. into Twelve divided, calld after the Names
> Of Israel: as they are in Eden. Mountain. River & Plain
> City & sandy Desart intermingled beyond mortal ken. (40:17–27, E141–142)

Ololon's speech 'sets her apart from the Shadowy Female, the sum of Rahab/Tirzah, who feared only that she herself would be consumed in Orc's consummation (18:25, 28). Ololon is no longer part of Rahab's jealous holiness' (Fox, 1976: 172).

Also feeling the effect of Ololon's words, Milton is compelled to speak again. Ololon has raised concerns about the children of Jerusalem. Returning to the theme of 'Self annihilation', Milton immediately connects his new State with saving the children. He then reverts to the vocabulary of the contraries and the Negation, which is identifiable with the Elect. He imparts to Ololon that the Negation must now be destroyed, and that this will be beneficial to the contraries: the Negation, identified with the Spectre in his speech, must be destroyed to 'redeem the Contraries' (40.33, E142). This is different from the earlier treatment of the Elect, connected to their being created continually. The destruction of the Negation proceeds along specific lines. It seems that the very different attitude to the Negation results from the fact that here the Negation is conceived of as a part of Milton's larger personality, which must be purified. Milton lists everything that must be 'cast off': the 'Not Human', the faculty of reason, memory, the 'infernal triad' (Damon, 1988: 298) of Bacon, Newton and Locke, who are spoken of metaphorically as Albion's garment, uninspired poetry, and the 'idiot Questioner', associated with publishing, who is beset by Despair and Envy (his Envy is a Wolf), who preaches 'Benevolence and Virtue' while condemning those who practise them. As the speech evolves, the element of vituperative becomes progressively more pronounced: Milton's voice blends with Blake's, and the speech begins to sounds more and more like Blakean verse diatribe. But to cast off all of these is not to cast off everything. The lesson of the Seven Angels was not wasted on Milton: he now knows, by virtue of his Humanity, that much can be preserved by annihilation: the Human, the imagination (rather than reason), faith (rather than doubt, the building block of Bacon's epistemology), and 'Inspiration'. His speech reaches a pitch of intensity when he identifies such figures as 'the destroyers of Jerusalem, ... the murderers/ Of Jesus'. Milton's speech evolves in this way, but at the outset, it is very obviously also a sociopolitical performative: addressing Ololon, he conveys the orders of the highest power. He will speak of his own self-annihilation, but it is clearly the case his speech is designed to carry illocutionary force geared towards Ololon's *emulating* his decisive action:

> But turning toward Ololon in terrible majesty Milton
> Replied. Obey thou the Words of the Inspired Man
> All that can be annihilated must be annihilated
> That the Children of Jerusalem may be saved from slavery
> There is a Negation, & there is a Contrary
> The Negation must be destroyd to redeem the Contraries
> The Negation is the Spectre; the Reasoning Power in Man
> This is a false Body: an Incrustation over my Immortal
> Spirit; a Selfhood, which must be put off & annihilated alway

114 *The Redemption of the Contraries*

> To cleanse the Face of my Spirit by Self-examination.
> To bathe in the Waters of Life; to wash off the Not Human
> I come in Self-annihilation & the grandeur of Inspiration
> To cast off Rational Demonstration by Faith in the Saviour
> To cast off the rotten rags of Memory by Inspiration
> To cast off Bacon, Locke & Newton from Albions covering
> To take off his filthy garments, & clothe him with Imagination
> To cast aside from Poetry, all that is not Inspiration
> That it no longer shall dare to mock with the aspersion of Madness
> Cast on the Inspired, by the tame high finisher of paltry Blots,
> Indefinite, or paltry Rhymes; or paltry Harmonies.
> Who creeps into State Government like a catterpiller to destroy
> To cast off the idiot Questioner who is always questioning,
> But never capable of answering; who sits with a sly grin
> Silent plotting when to question, like a thief in a cave;
> Who publishes doubt & calls it knowledge; whose Science is Despair
> Whose pretence to knowledge is Envy, whose whole Science is
> To destroy the wisdom of ages to gratify ravenous Envy;
> That rages round him like a Wolf day & night without rest
> He smiles with condescension; he talks of Benevolence & Virtue
> And those who act with Benevolence & Virtue, they murder time on time
> These are the destroyers of Jerusalem, these are the murderers
> Of Jesus, who deny the Faith & mock at Eternal Life:
> Who pretend to Poetry that they may destroy Imagination;
> By imitation of Natures Images drawn from Remembrance
> These are the Sexual Garments, the Abomination of Desolation
> Hiding the Human lineaments as with an Ark & Curtains
> Which Jesus rent: & now shall wholly purge away with Fire
> Till Generation is swallowd up in Regeneration. (40.28–41.28, E142–3)

His performative pronouncement results in further consolidation of the instant. In spite of its august tone, his speech results in a non-combative verbal response from Ololon, which combined with the force of Milton's words, starts to produce a physical effect, which begins to register before Ololon even concludes her response. Ololon's journey has prepared her for Milton's statement about the Negation and the contraries: we remember that she reached a place where the contraries of Beulah engage in warfare under the Negation's standard

(34.23, E134). She shows her understanding of the fact that she is a female-will figure, and that, while in Eden a unity of male and female principles is stable, those living a sexual existence in Beulah find that their lower paradise opens downwards to the depths of Ulro, such is the precariousness of that existence. She is explicit about her and Milton's being contraries, and, harking back to the image of Milton struggling with his sixfold emanation (the 'conflict with those Female Forms'), she suggests that their struggle has been like the wars of time. (In the design accompanying the text (plate 44 (43)), it is as though the sixfold emanation is slowly becoming a unity.) She understands the significance of Eternal Death, and concludes that she must follow Milton's example and embrace it. By this time, she has started to separate herself from the female will, but that refers only to the casting off of her Rahab side, and Ololon is more than this. In the second chapter, I turned to Frye for an understanding of the different types of symbolically male and female principles which structure Blake's thought. In another iteration of the idea, Frye states that 'there are two aspects of the object: the retreating elusive object and the responding or transformed object. Blake calls the former the "Female Will" and the latter the "Emanation", the total body of what one redeems by love' (2005a: 415). Her degenerate aspect, a 'Double Six-fold Wonder,' then unites with Milton's Shadow as his Shadow's Emanation:

> Is this our Femin[in]e Portion the Six-fold Miltonic Female
> Terribly this Portion trembles before thee O awful Man
> Altho' our Human Power can sustain the severe contentions
> Of Friendship, our Sexual cannot: but flies into the Ulro.
> Hence arose all our terrors in Eternity! & now remembrance
> Returns upon us! are we Contraries O Milton, Thou & I
> O Immortal! how were we led to War the Wars of Death
> Is this the Void Outside of Existence, which if enterd into
> Becomes a Womb? & is this the Death Couch of Albion
> Thou goest to Eternal Death & all must go with thee
>
> So saying, the Virgin divided Six-fold & with a shriek
> Dolorous that ran thro all Creation a Double Six-fold Wonder!
> Away from Ololon she divided & fled into the depths
> Of Miltons Shadow as a Dove upon the stormy Sea. (41.30–42.6, E143)

This is the last speech in the poem, and as Fox argues, '[Ololon's] last speech is simply the temporal manifestation of the Edenic situation in the first' (1976: 180). She continues,

This last speech of Ololon ends with her division from Rahab, even as her speech two plates earlier did ... The dramatic difference between the earlier representation of the division and this one is that between the speeches Milton has turned toward Ololon. Now when Rahab divides from her, there is nothing to prevent her union with Milton. (1976: 181)

Her shriek is both a shriek of terror and of birth (Bloom, 1982: 927). Frye states that at this point, 'the bride Ololon, purified of the stain of virginity, stands before the poet in his final consummation' (2004: 345). 'Ololon is united with Milton in the image of a new birth' (1976: 116), states James. Turning to the design on plate 46(45), he continues: 'This birth is also copulation, and the sexual encounter or "loss of virginity" synonymous with union is pictured in a full-page illustration towards the end of the poem' (ibid.). Milton's 'doctrine of chastity' (Wittreich, 1975: 247) is overcome.

Finale

Blake does not dwell on this image. Rather, he emphasizes the phenomenological power of the dialogue between Milton and Ololon. At this stage, his focus is the larger significance of Milton's successful uniting with his emanation, Ololon. The finale is non-verbal, but it can be seen as the perlocutionary effect of the speech discussed in this chapter.

As we have seen, Ololon is associated with 'Clouds' in connection with Jesus (21.58–59, E116). Now Christ appears when Ololon as a 'Moony Ark' descends into the 'Fires of Intellect' (42.9, E143). Milton is identifiable as the 'Eighth/ Image Divine' (15.5–16.5, E109), but the 'Starry Eight' (42.10, E143) are identical with Christ: they become 'One Man/ Jesus the Saviour' (42.11, E143). As Fox states:

> Ironically, Milton appears as Satan in his descent, Ololon as Jesus in hers. The heroic prophet seems an Elect tyrant, the meek sufferer seems the Reprobate savior. This surprising division exists not because Ololon is purer than Milton, but because her act completes his and thus perfects their union. Milton, after all, however satanic he seems, is himself the eighth Eye of God, a form of Jesus even as Ololon is a form of Jesus; the union of the eight with Ololon is the fulfillment of the eight, the act by which they, not just she, become Jesus. For Blake to say here that Jesus appears with Ololon is to imply that Ololon and Milton are united in their descent. (1976: 94)

The Redemption of the Contraries 117

Ololon descends in 'clouds of blood, streams of gore' (42.8, E143), and the clouds clothe Jesus: 'round his limbs/ The Clouds of Ololon folded as a Garment dipped in blood' (42.11–12, E143). The 'Clouds of Blood' is a garment which represents the wars of human history. It is a metaphor appertaining to the area of demonic imagery and unites an image of the world of water (the cloud) with an image of 'the human' (blood). Its apocalyptic counterpart is 'the river of fresh water' alluded to in Revelation (22:1), which, as Frye explains, represents the 'circulating blood of man's risen body' (2005a: 247). Its lineage includes related demonic images such as the water that gushes from Christ's side when his crucified body is pierced by the Holy Lance.

What is the significance of the fact that the 'Clouds of blood' clothe Christ? Crucially, the 'clouds of blood' are identified with something verbal in the poem, and we need to think of Jesus as the Word of God as well. One of Blake's sources is explicit about this latter point: 'And he was clothed with a vesture dipped in blood: and his name is called The Word of God' (Revelation: 19:13). Importantly, the Word of God is not a self-referring word, nor a mirror held up to human life. Rather, much of the history of human endeavour is *contained* in this Word. As Frye explains, the poem demands of us that we think of 'all efforts of human culture and civilization' (2004: 332) as part of the genuine Word of God.

Of course human history is much more than this: history has been characterized by innumerable wars and human suffering. In connection with this, it is also made clear in the poem that the clouds, this garment, the history of warfare, is also a Word, 'Divine Revelation in the Litteral Expression' (42.14, E143). As Frye clarifies, if human life is to be thought of in terms of the Word of God, then clearly most of human life is part of an impostor Word, which matches the 'scripture' perverted by what Blake calls the 'corporeal understanding' – history as warfare is part of the scripture produced by literalism.

The 'clouds of blood' which, like a garment, clothe Christ, clearly represent this bloody history of mankind. In a composite image, then, which seems to embody all of history, be it culture and civilization or warfare, in the poem's finale *one Word clothes another*.

Prior to the very end of the poem, we return to the figure of Albion trying to rouse himself: this time, it is as though he is reacting to the emerging defeat of Satan. He begins to rise from his slumbers, although he quickly sinks down again, too weak to rise properly (39.32–52, E140–141). At the very end of the poem, Blake sees Albion's cities, twenty-four in number, take up their thrones, from where they are to judge the nations. They appear in the four zoas, who now rise around Albion's body. The developments culminate in what Damon calls the 'mystical ecstasy' (1988: 280). Jesus, passing from the above scene in Felpham, still clothed in 'Clouds of Blood', enters Albion's bosom, the zoas surrounding him *in* 'the Fires of Intellect' (42.9, E143). Lastly, the zoas apply trumpets to their lips and sound the trumpets to the four winds.

References

Blake, W. (1988), *The Complete Poetry and Prose of William Blake: Newly Revised Edition*, ed. D. V. Erdman, University of California Press: Berkeley.

Bloom, H. (1982), 'Commentary', in *The Complete Poetry and Prose of William Blake*, ed. D.V. Erdman, Berkeley: University of California Press, 894–972.

Damon, S.F. (1988), *A Blake Dictionary: The Ideas and Symbols of William Blake*, Hanover: University Press of New England.

Fox, S. (1976), *Poetic Form in Blake's Milton*, Princeton: Princeton University Press.

Frye, N. (2004), *Fearful Symmetry: A Study of William Blake*, ed. N. Halmi, Toronto: University of Toronto Press.

Frye, N. (2005a), *Northrop Frye on Milton and Blake*, ed. A. Esterhammer, Toronto: University of Toronto Press.

Frye, N. (2006), *The Great Code: The Bible and Literature*, ed. A.A. Lee, Toronto: University of Toronto Press.

Howard, J. (1976), *Blake's Milton: A Study in Selfhood*, London: Associated University Presses.

James, D. (1977), *Written Within and Without: A Study of Blake's Milton*, Frankfurt: Peter Lang.

Matthews, L. (1980), '"The Value of the Savior's Blood": The Idea of Atonement in Blake's *Milton*', *Wascana Review*, LV (Spring): 72–86.

Summerfield, H. (1998), *A Guide to the Books of William Blake for Innocent and Experienced Readers*, Gerrards Cross: Colin Smythe.

Wittreich, J. (1975), *Angel of Apocalypse: Blake's Idea of Milton*, Wisconsin: University of Wisconsin.

7 Coda: *Milton* as Speech Act

Blake faints under the burden of the vision. The focus then returns to the image of the lark (the twenty-eighth) in Felpham's Vale and the Wild Thyme, and then to how Los and Enitharmon rise over the hills of Surrey. Contemporary England is spoken of in connection with the endeavours of Oothoon and Los: the Human Harvest is hers, and Los is wrathful over the human condition in London. 'Just before his head clears', says Frye, 'Blake gets a fleeting glimpse of still another vision' (2004: 355). The last vision is that of Rintrah and Palamabron, and the imagery harks back to the time when Los-Blake-Milton encounter the sons of Luvah at the winepress, and beyond that to the Bard's Song.

Upon the completion of our reading of the poem, the issue of the role of the reader becomes significant. More particularly, what of the poem as whole as a speech act? What kind of effect does it have on the reader?

Approaching this question, it will be useful if we first consider the narrator, and, before that, the difference between the intradiegetic Blake's vision and the orbit for that vision. The vision experienced by the intradiegetic Blake is *part of* the last possible 'instant' before apocalypse. The rest of the instant represents the orbit of that vision. Additionally, I think we might confidently conclude that the events related in the Bard's Song, though I have spoken of them as prior to the instant, are also part of the larger orbit of Blake's vision.

At the very beginning of this study, I hinted at a distinction between two perspectives, one which is 'in time', the other which is 'beyond time'. In connection with the latter, Fox speaks of 'the consciousness that does not recognize calibrated duration', which is 'beyond our realm of decades and centuries' (1976: 16).[1] Blake-as-narrator enjoys this perspective. What he can see is his own earlier visionary experience and the full orbit of it, which includes, again, the rest of the instant *and* the sacred history preceding it, provided by the Bard's Song. Speaking of the poem, Frye astutely observes that

DOI: 10.4324/9781003342571-8

120 Coda: Milton as Speech Act

'What is said, so to speak, in the text of *Milton* is designed to present the context of the illuminated moment as a single simultaneous pattern of apprehension', and Blake's visionary experience 'links him with a series of previous moments stretching back to the creation of the world' (2005a: 318–319). It might be useful to assume that in order to share that vision with the reader, the narrator must engage in a process which is the reverse of what (as I shall explain) the reader must do. The narrator must change what he sees as a 'structure' into something closer to narrative. Given the extent to which *Milton* is atypical as a narrative poem, it will be safer to say that the narrator changes the picture before him into what Frye (in a theoretical context) calls 'movement in time', something which can be read sequentially.

Ultimately, the reader of *Milton* strives to see what the narrator can see – to share in his vision – and is enabled by the narrator to do so: the narrator provides us with a sequence we can make our way through in time, so that at the end we may see as he sees. 'Movement in time' is Frye's phrase for reading: 'The first thing that confronts us in studying verbal structures is that they are arranged sequentially, and have to be read or listened to in time' (Frye, 2006: 49). At the end of the process, however, there is an 'arrest of time'. As we process what we have read, we hopefully begin 'to see'; what emerges is more like a spatial art than one which moves in time like music:

> Once a verbal structure is read, and reread often enough to be possessed, it "freezes". It turns into a unity in which all parts exist at once, without regard to the specific movement of the narrative. [...] The term "structure" [...] is a metaphor from architecture, and may be misleading when we are speaking of narrative, which is not a simultaneous structure but a movement in time. The term "structure" comes into its proper context in the second stage, which is where all discussion of "spatial form" and kindred critical topics take their origin. (Frye, 2006: 81)

If we look back over the ground we have covered, it is not difficult to rehearse what that reader's vision is like, once s/he has attained the perspective of the narrator. In the foreground, as it were, we have Milton's struggle with Satan, along with Milton's uniting with Ololon and the vision of Golgonooza enjoyed by Los-Blake-Milton. Beyond that, we have the descent of Ololon, the resistance of the Sons of Luvah as well as Rintrah and Palamabron to Los-Blake-Milton during the journey to Golgonooza, the resistance to Milton's redeemed self on

Coda: Milton as Speech Act 121

the part of Tirzah and Rahab, as well as the zoas and, to an extent, their emanations, the process whereby Milton's person gets disaggregated into its separate parts, Milton's first hearing the Bard's Song, and all the events of the Bard's Song from Luetha giving birth to Death and various female-will figures all the way back to Luvah's assuming the world of Urizen in the south. This commentary has highlighted the extent to which the important acts of this structure are verbal: it is permeated by language use.

We might finish by going back to the one of the most discussed features of the poem: the notion of Milton freeing Orc from the 'Chain of Jealousy', which may be suggested by the symbol of the Eighth Eye. Blake scholarship exhibits a wide range of different views regarding whether or not the liberation of Orc is an organic part of the poem. Those who do think Orc is freed by Milton's descent and self-sacrifice have advanced a variety of theories about when this happens and what it entails.[2]

My own argument about the poem as a speech act suggests a different conclusion about the freeing of Orc. Frye suggests that the great Romantic theme is the attainment of vision, and that the vision tends to be *individual* in the poetry of the period. 'Such an event, taking place in an individual consciousness, may become a sign of a greater social awakening, but the latter is usually implied in it or takes place offstage' (2005b: 117). The freeing of Orc in *Milton* should be connected to the notion of a 'greater social awakening', of which Blake's own enlightenment is the harbinger. Paley suggests that *Milton* is flawed in this respect. 'Evidently Blake had once thought of bringing together the internal-regenerative and the external-millennial elements of the poem in the co-operation of Milton and Orc. This was not to be carried further' (2011: 802). But my own reading of the poem suggests that the reader may see as the narrator sees, which means that the vision set forth in the poem can be shared and passed on. The reader's having the same vision as Blake the narrator is a possible perlocutionary effect of the poem as a whole. And of course in proportion as the vision is spread through reading, the vision goes from being individual to social – and Orc is freed. '*Milton*', observes Frye, 'is an individual prologue to the omen of something universal coming on (2004: 316–317). Frye has in mind Blake's next epic, *Jerusalem*, in which the focus is the social, although the result is 'a less completely concentrated poem partly because of its attempt at a wider social vision' (2005b: 117). But the universal thing coming on might equally be the vision afforded by the reader response to *Milton*. Cogan reaches a similar conclusion: 'If it is the job of prophets to open our eyes to these glimpses of the eternal, for the first time in his poetry in *Milton* Blake attempts to enact this not by declaiming his visionary oracles but by sharing with us what it is like to see as a visionary. In this way, Blake attempts to extend the visionary *parousia* to include the reader through the medium of the text' (2021: 188).[3] It may well be that Orc is freed from the Chain, although that liberation depends on a collective response to poem as speech act, which, in Frye's metaphor, occurs 'offstage'.

Notes

1 The distinction I rehearse here may help to explain something of an ambiguity in Fox's commentary. At times she is unequivocal about the fact that the events related in the Bard's Song predate the 'instant' which much of the poem is dedicated to exploring. But at times she suggests that the events of the Bard's Song are also simultaneous with everything else in the poem. Thus when speaking of how the repeated narrative return to Albion's stirring in his sleep indicates the simultaneity of the action, she includes a development which is related in the Bard's Song – Los's altering the poles of the world (9.17, E103) – and seemed to *precede* the instant: 'Once again the poem's simultaneity is clarified: the sons of Los call on Albion to wake and then watch as he turns and falls back into sleep – the same turn Blake himself noted three plates earlier, attributing it not to the exhortations of Rintrah and Palamabron, but to the "electric flame of Miltons awful precipitate descent" ... . Thus Milton's descent and the exhortations provoked by his arrival in Blake's person at Golgonooza are simultaneous. The cries of Rintrah and Palamabron and "the sounds of War" Albion hears are by this simultaneity identified with Los's wrath as he alters the poles of the world, with the groans of the eternals as Milton descends, with the anguish of Orc as he battles his Shadowy Female, and with the lamentations of Jesus and Ololon at her descent' (1976: 100). It may well be that it comes down to a question of whether we view the events as part of the reading process and 'movement in time', or whether we are seeing them as part of the structure which emerges as we develop our understanding after reading.
2 For a succinct account of decades about disagreement about this feature of the poem, see Summerfield 635–636.
3 Cogan then comments 'This mirrors Ricœur's conception of a mutually transformative hermeneutics in which the world of the text and the world of the reader combine and remake one another' (2021: 188), but we are provided with no further explanation of how Ricœur's work helps us with this crucial point.

References

Blake, W. (1988), *The Complete Poetry and Prose of William Blake: Newly Revised Edition*, ed. D. V. Erdman, University of California Press: Berkeley.
Cogan, L. (2021), *Blake and the Failure of Prophecy*, Houndmills: Palgrave.
Fox, S. (1976), *Poetic Form in Blake's Milton*, Princeton: Princeton University Press.

Frye, N. (2004), *Fearful Symmetry: A Study of William Blake*, ed.N. Halmi, Toronto: University of Toronto Press.

Frye, N. (2005a), *Northrop Frye on Milton and Blake*, ed.A. Esterhammer, Toronto: University of Toronto Press.

Frye, N. (2005b), *Northrop Frye's Writings on the Eighteenth and Nineteenth Centuries*, ed. I. Salusinsky, Toronto: University of Toronto Press.

Frye, N. (2006), *The Great Code: The Bible and Literature*, ed. A.A. Lee, Toronto: University of Toronto Press.

Paley, M. (2011), 'William Blake's *Milton/A Poem* and the Miltonic Matrix of 1791–1810'. *University of Toronto Quarterly* 80.4. (2011): 786–814.

Bibliography

Apesos, A. (2015), 'The Poet in the Poem: Blake's *Milton*', *Studies in Philology* 112.2: 379–413.
Blake, W. (1988), *The Complete Poetry and Prose of William Blake: Newly Revised Edition*, ed. D. V. Erdman, University of California Press: Berkeley.
Bloom, H. (1982), 'Commentary', in *The Complete Poetry and Prose of William Blake*, ed. D.V. Erdman, Berkeley: University of California Press, 894–972.
Bracher, M. (1985), *Being Form'd: Thinking Through Blake's Milton*, New York: Statin Hill Press.
Cogan, L. (2021), *Blake and the Failure of Prophecy*, Houndmills: Palgrave.
Damon, S.F. ([1924] 1958), *William Blake: His Philosophy and Symbols*, Gloucester, MA: Peter Smith.
Damon, S.F. (1988), *A Blake Dictionary: The Ideas and Symbols of William Blake*, Hanover: University Press of New England.
De Luca, V.A. (1991), *Words of Eternity: Blake and the Poetics of the Sublime*, Princeton: Princeton University Press.
Eaves, M. (2012), 'Afterword: The End? Remember Me!', in *Re-envisioning Blake*, eds. M. Crosby, T. Patenaude and A. Whitehead, Houndmills: Palgrave, 225–231.
Erdman, D. (1965), Blake's *Jerusalem*: Plate 3 Fully Restored', *Studies in Bibliography* XVIII: 281–282.
Erdman, D. (1969), *Prophet Against Empire: A Poet's Interpretation of the History of His Own Times*, Princeton: Princeton University Press.
Essick, R. and J. Viscomi. (1993), *Milton: A Poem and the Final Illuminated Works, The Ghost of Abel, On Homer's Poetry, On Virgil's Laocoön*, ed. W. Blake, Princeton: William Blake Trust/Princeton University Press.
Essick, R.N. (1989), *William Blake and the Language of Adam*, Oxford: Clarendon Press.
Esterhammer, A. (1994), *Creating States: Studies in the Performative Language of John Milton and William Blake*, Toronto: University of Toronto Press.
Fallon, D. (2017), *Blake, Myth, and Enlightenment: The Politics of Apotheosis*, Houndmills: Palgrave.

Fox, S. (1976), *Poetic Form in Blake's Milton*, Princeton: Princeton University Press.

Frye, N. (1990), *Words With Power: Being A Second Study of the Bible and Literature*, New York: A Harvest/HBJ Book.

Frye, N. (2004), *Fearful Symmetry: A Study of William Blake*, ed. N. Halmi, Toronto: University of Toronto Press.

Frye, N. (2005a), *Northrop Frye on Milton and Blake*, ed. A. Esterhammer, Toronto: University of Toronto Press.

Frye, N. (2005b), *Northrop Frye's Writings on the Eighteenth and Nineteenth Centuries*, ed. I. Salusinsky, Toronto: University of Toronto Press.

Frye, N. (2006), *The Great Code: The Bible and Literature*, ed. A.A. Lee, Toronto: University of Toronto Press.

Hilton, N. (1983), *Literal Imagination: Blake's Vision of Words*, Berkeley: University of California Press.

Howard, J. (1976), *Blake's Milton: A Study in Selfhood*, London: Associated University Presses.

James, D. (1977), *Written Within and Without: A Study of Blake's Milton*, Frankfurt: Peter Lang.

Jones, J.H. (2010), *Blake on Language, Power, and Self-Annihilation*, Houndmills: Palgrave.

Matthews, L. (1980), '"The Value of the Savior's Blood": The Idea of Atonement in Blake's *Milton*', *Wascana Review*, LV (Spring): 72–86.

Paley, M. (1970), *Energy and the Imagination: A Study of the Development of Blake's Thought*, Oxford: Clarendon Press.

Paley, M. (2011), 'William Blake's *Milton/A Poem* and the Miltonic Matrix of 1791–1810', *University of Toronto Quarterly* 80.4: 786–814.

Petry, S. (2016), *Speech Acts and Literary Theory*, London: Routledge.

Riede, D.G. (1991), *Oracles and Hierophants: Constructions of Romantic Authority*, Ithaca: Cornell University Press.

Rieger, J. (1973), '"The Hem of Their Garments": The Bard's Song in *Milton*', in *Blake's Sublime Allegory*, Madison: University of Wisconsin, 259–280.

Rix, D.S. (1984), '*Milton*: Blake's Reading of the Second Isaiah', in *Poetic Prophecy in Western Literature*, ed. J. Wojcik and R. Frontain, London: Associated University Press, 106–118.

Summerfield, H. (1998), *A Guide to the Books of William Blake for Innocent and Experienced Readers*, Gerrards Cross: Colin Smythe.

Sutherland, J.H. (1977), 'Blake's *Milton*: The Bard's Song', *CLQ*, XIII, 142–157.

Taylor, R.C. (1979), 'Semantic Structures and the Temporal Modes of Blake's Prophetic Verse', *Language and Style* 12: 26–49.

Williams. N. (ed.) (2006), *Palgrave Advances in William Blake Studies*, Houndmills: Palgrave.

Wittreich, J. (1975), *Angel of Apocalypse: Blake's Idea of Milton*, Wisconsin: University of Wisconsin.

Index

Page numbers followed by "n" indicate notes.

Adam 42, 54
Ahania 62, 63
Albion 19–20, 24, 37, 41, 43, 54, 57, 62, 63, 70, 72, 73, 74, 75, 77, 80, 84, 87, 110, 113, 117–118, 122n1
anagnorisis 24–25, 69
Apesos, Anthony 101
Apocalypse 1, 2, 3, 11, 12, 13, 14, 15, 18, 41, 69–70, 74, 75, 77, 86, 88, 91, 119
Aristotle 24
Austin, J.L. 4, 7, 13, 15–16n2

Bacon, Francis 62, 113, 114
Bakhtin, Mikhail 13
Bard's Song 1, 2, 3, 4, 5, 6, 11, 13, 14, 18–19, 22–33, 34–50, 55, 103, 104, 119, 121, 122n1
Beulah 15, 21, 25, 30, 40, 45, 53, 54, 55, 61, 73, 83, 94–96, 99, 100, 114
Blake, Catherine 101
Blake, William (in *Milton*), in Felpham 1, 2, 75, 88, 99, 101–102, 103–118, 119–122; in Golgonooza 1, 3, 5, 14–15, 119–122, 122n1; journey to Golgonooza 5, 14–15, 91, 119; narrator 18, 37, 101, 105, 119–122; sees Milton falling 54; unites with Los (after Milton has united with Blake) 1, 91, 65, 66–69, 101
Blake, William (author), Druidism, mathematics and rationalism 24; 'And did those feet' or 'Jerusalem' 19, 25; *Europe* 1; *The (First) Book of Urizen* 22; *The Four Zoas* 20, 22, 76; *Jerusalem* 5, 22, 52, 69, 121; *The Marriage of Heaven and Hell* 71; nature (view of) 45–49; 'On Homers Poetry' 6; 'On Virgil' 6; performative features of his poetry 8–12; rejection of violence (embrace of intellectual battle) 3–6; *Songs of Innocence and Experience* 10; *There is No Natural Religion* 45, 46; view of intellectual conflict *versus* war 5–6; *A Vision of the Last Judgement* 11; war (view of) 48–49, 70, 86; works other than *Milton* 1, 5, 6, 10, 11, 19, 20, 22, 25, 45, 46, 52, 69, 71, 76, 121
Bloom, Harold 35, 55, 58, 61–62, 72, 116
Bracher, Mark 56, 59, 60, 66

Canaan 31, 61, 63, 64, 112
Chain of Jealousy 62, 63, 121–122
Charles II 35
Cogan, Lucy 13, 16n6, 68, 121–122, 122n3
Contraries 113–118
Covering Cherub 40, 59, 72, 74, 77, 79, 104
Cromwell, Oliver 35, 62

Daughters of Beulah 18, 37, 47, 94
Damon, S.F. 3, 41–42, 46, 76, 77, 84, 113, 118
Death 13, 18, 34, 36, 40, 44, 60, 96, 97, 110, 121
Deism 14, 41, 48–49, 50, 62, 63, 111
Druidism 23–24, 31, 62

Eaves, Morris 8
Eden 5, 6, 12, 15, 21–22, 25, 30, 45, 53–54, 76, 78, 92–94, 96, 99, 107, 112
Elect 34–35, 42, 87, 88–89
Elynittria 36–40
Emanation 19, 20, 22, 39, 44–47, 52, 54, 57, 58, 60, 62, 103
Enion 62, 63
Enitharmon 14, 20, 22, 23, 30–31, 52, 57–58, 63, 80, 82, 97, 119
epic 6, 7
Erdman, David V. 50
Essick, Robert N. 8, 15n1
Esterhammer, Angela 8–11, 13
Eyes of God or Angels of the Presence 2, 6, 40–41, 42, 53, 75, 78, 92, 97–98, 100, 106–109, 110, 113, 116, 121

Fabula (of *Milton*) 18–19, 20, 42
Fall 1, 13, 14, 18, 20–21, 22, 24–33, 34–42, 76, 79, 84
female will 31, 46–47, 48, 55, 57, 115, 121
Fox, Susan 1–3, 8, 11–12, 57, 60, 68–69, 70, 72, 85, 94, 96, 98, 99, 101, 104, 110, 112, 116, 119, 122n1
Four Zoas 5, 14, 20, 30, 42, 56, 62, 79, 80, 85, 110, 111, 118, 121
Frye, Northrop 3, 7, 8, 9, 19, 21, 23, 24–25, 27, 31, 32, 41, 42, 44, 45, 46, 47, 48, 49, 61, 68, 71, 84, 85, 94, 96, 103, 107, 109, 115, 116, 117, 119, 120, 121, 122

Generation 12, 22, 30
Golgonooza 1, 14, 15, 19, 22, 56, 61, 64, 65, 66, 69, 70, 75, 91, 98–102, 104, 121, 122n1; Allamanda 77, 79, 80, 81, 82, 84–85, 87; Bowlahoola 70, 73, 74, 77, 79–85; 'Fountain in a rock' 99–100; Lark 99–100; 'rock of Odours' 99–100; 'Wild Thyme' 99–100; Wine-press 78, 80, 85–86, 119

Hellenic *versus* Hebraic 6, 39, 47, 62
Hilton, Nelson 89
History (sacred) 40–42, 77
Homer 81
Howard, John 24, 32–33, 60, 68, 93–94, 106, 110

James, David E. 4, 8, 29, 49, 92, 94, 95, 96, 107, 116
James I. 35
Jerusalem 19, 20, 23, 24, 37, 60, 62, 71, 73, 84, 87–88, 89, 94, 97, 113, 114
Jesus 2–3, 11, 12, 35, 41, 42, 43, 62, 63, 79, 88, 89, 93, 94–95, 98, 113, 116–118, 122n1; as the Word of God 86, 117
Jones J.H. 13, 28, 16n6

Lewis, C.S. 7
Locke, John 25, 46, 113, 114
Los 1, 3, 4, 5, 6, 14, 15, 18, 22, 23, 24–33, 39, 41, 57–58, 60, 63, 66, 67–69, 69–79, 80, 82, 84, 85, 87, 92, 94, 97, 98, 99–100, 101, 110, 119, 120, 122n1
Luetha 6, 14, 35–42, 60, 121
Luvah 4, 5, 15, 30, 120, 121

Middleton, Peter 8
Milton (in *Milton*), body (of Milton in the poem) 53, 56, 65, 66; confronts Satan in Felpham 1, 4, 11, 14–15, 103–111, 119; descends into Felpham 103, 104; Eighth Eye 41, 65, 92, 95–96, 97–98, 101, 116; Elect self of 66, 75, 76, 77, 78, 79; emanation of 11–12, 14, 15, 47, 53, 55, 91, 94, 103, 105, 111, 115; freeing of Orc 121–122; Humanity 53, 56, 65, 67, 103; in heaven 6, 11, 13, 18, 40, 43, 50; initial descent of 92, 95; journey of redeemed self 4, 14, 52, 55, 56, 57–64, 65, 120; physical struggle with Urizen (on the part of redeemed self) 3–4,

65, 105, 111; Shadow of 53–55, 57, 61, 72, 103, 104, 115; speaks to and unites with Ololon in Felpham 4, 6, 103–118, 119; Spectre of 14, 44, 53, 54, 66, 103–111; unites and journeys with Blake and Los to Golgonooza 5, 14–15, 65, 66–69, 94, 119; wives and daughters of 47, 55–56, 62, 94, 96
Milton, John (author), Cromwell (view of) 62; *Comus* 101; 'On His Deceased Wife' (Sonnet XXIII) 47; *Paradise Lost* 3, 18, 36, 49, 103; Puritanism of 14, 48–49, 50, 62, 71, 73; Satan and Messiah of 29; works 3, 18, 36, 47, 49, 101, 103
Mundane Egg and Shell 41, 99, 104

Negation 113, 114
Newton, Isaac 24, 25, 46, 111, 113, 114
Orc 14, 15, 20, 22, 30, 40–41, 57, 58–60, 61, 73, 74, 94, 121–122
Ololon 1–2, 4, 6, 11, 12, 15, 68, 91–102, 103–4, 106, 111–118, 119, 120, 122n1

Paine, Thomas 24
Palamabron 3, 5, 14, 18, 24–33, 34–35, 36–38, 40, 57, 69–79, 81, 86, 87, 104, 119, 120, 122n1
Paley, Morton 42, 48–49, 86, 121
Pity and wrath 18, 31–33
Polypus 41, 53, 81, 96, 98, 101, 104

Rahab 1, 4, 40, 55, 56, 57, 59, 60–64, 70, 72, 76, 82, 94, 97, 103, 111, 115–116, 112, 121
Reader of *Milton* 119–122
Redeemed 34–35, 41, 42, 87, 88–89
Reprobate 35, 42, 87, 88–89
Ricœr, Paul 13, 122n3
Rieger, James 27, 29
Rintrah 3, 5, 14, 18, 24–33, 34–35, 57, 69–79, 81, 86, 87, 104, 119, 120, 122n1
Rix, Donna S. 31–32

Romanticism 9, 121
Rousseau, Jean-Jacques 70, 72, 73, 111

Satan 1, 3, 4–5, 11, 14, 15, 18, 20, 21, 22, 24–33, 34–35, 36–39, 42, 43, 44, 53, 54, 57, 59, 70, 73, 75, 77, 80, 84, 99, 100, 103–111, 116, 117, 120
Shadowy Female 14, 20, 23, 30, 57, 58–60, 70, 94, 122n1
Shakespeare, William 62
Shelley, Percy Bysshe 45, 69, 105
simultaneity of action in *Milton* 1–3, 11–12, 13, 42–43, 57, 98, 119–121, 122n1
Sin 13, 18, 34, 36–39, 44, 110
space 13, 18, 30–33, 82–84
spectre(s) 20, 22, 23, 30, 31, 44, 47, 52, 82
speech act theory 8–12, 13
Summerfield, Henry 94, 106, 122n2
Swedenborg, Emanuel 71, 73
Syuzet (of *Milton*) 18, 22, 42

Taylor, R.C. 8, 50
Tharmas 21, 58, 80
'Three classes of men' 18, 34, 35, 44, 52, 82
'Three Heavens of Beulah' 55, 56, 61
Tirzah 4, 14, 40, 56, 57, 59, 60–64, 71, 72, 76, 82, 97, 103, 111, 121
time 13, 18, 34, 40–42, 82–84
Twenty-Seven Churches or Heavens 40–42, 53, 61, 76, 100, 103
two perspectives on time in *Milton* 1, 119–122

Ulro 6, 15, 30–31, 40, 56, 73, 76, 79, 92, 95–98
Urizen 3–4, 14, 21, 22, 23, 24, 30, 57, 58, 60, 61, 64, 80, 121
Urthona 42

Vala 62, 63
Viscomi, Joseph 15n1
Voltaire 70, 72, 73, 111

Wittreich, Joseph A. 8, 49, 116, 16n3